NET

RESULTS

NET

RESULTS

Great Fishing Spots in Southern Wisconsin

Bob Riepenhoff

The University of Wisconsin Press

The University of Wisconsin Press
1930 Monroe Street
Madison, Wisconsin 53711

www.wisc.edu/wisconsinpress/

3 Henrietta Street
London WC2E 8LU, England

Library of Congress Cataloging-in-Publication Data
Riepenhoff, Bob.
Net results : great fishing spots in southern Wisconsin / Bob Riepenhoff ;
foreword by Don L. Johnson
p. cm.
ISBN 0-299-19844-8 (pbk. : alk. paper)
1. Fishing—Wisconsin—Milwaukee Region. 2. Freshwater fishes—
Wisconsin—Milwaukee Region. 3. Lakes—Wisconsin—Milwaukee Region.
I. Title.
SH563.R54   2004
799.1'1'097759—dc22   2004012630

Contents

Foreword

Wisconsin has nearly fifteen thousand lakes, including many that are sited in pristine wilderness areas in the north. But this book is not about those. Instead, it is about lakes which, more often than not, are virtually surrounded by mankind's development.

Surprisingly though, waters within a few hours' drive of Milwaukee remain productive, hard-fished though they may be. In fact, many offer better fishing today than they did decades ago, not only for bass, northern pike, and panfish, but—if you choose the right time and place—even for walleyes, trout, and the mighty musky.

The first book describing favorite fishing spots near Milwaukee was published by the *Milwaukee Journal* in the early 1950s. It was a collection of stories which had appeared in the paper under the byline of my old friend, the late Mel Ellis, then the Outdoor Editor of the *Journal*.

That book proved popular, as did a succession of others as the *Journal's* outdoor desk was staffed by Tom Guyant, Jay Reed, and Ron Leys. Ron is long retired and Tom and Jay have gone to a place where the fish always bite.

The *Journal's* last fishing book, now long out of print, was authored by Ron Leys and Dick Smith, the latter a fishing guide in southeastern Wisconsin. That was in 1989. Things have changed since then, often for the better.

The void has now been filled by Bob Riepenhoff, Outdoor Editor of what is now the *Milwaukee Journal Sentinel*. Bob has been to far and exotic places during his fourteen years at the outdoors desk, but excitement is still apparent in his prose as he tells of battling a Lake Beulah bass or a Pewaukee Lake musky.

This is a book long overdue, written by the man best able to tell it like it is. Bob Riepenhoff describes lake structure, as well as the techniques and tackle found effective by knowledgeable anglers on specific lakes. He has included information from the Department of Natural Resources on fish stockings, special regulations, creel surveys, and fish population studies. And the maps, showing lake bottom contours, access points, and boat rental availability, are especially helpful.

Altogether, I think you'll agree it's a fine job, and one which seems sure to help you catch more fish. Tight lines!

DON L. JOHNSON
RETIRED *MILWAUKEE SENTINEL* OUTDOOR WRITER

Preface

Southern Wisconsin abounds with fishing opportunities.

In fourteen years as Outdoor Editor with the old *Milwaukee Journal* and now the *Milwaukee Journal Sentinel*, it has been my privilege to spend countless hours fishing with some of the most skilled anglers in the state. Mostly with their guidance, I fished the best-known, top-producing, most heavily fished lakes, as well as some quiet little spots where you can get away from the crowd for a little peace and serenity. Our time on the water followed the cycle of the seasons. We caught all kinds of fish, from bluegills to muskies, using a wide variety of techniques, both in open water and through the ice.

I'd like to thank the anglers whose hard-earned fishing knowledge and generosity of spirit have helped me keep on top of Wisconsin's fishing scene, week after week, and, to a large extent, helped make this book possible. The regulars are Don Streeter, Steve Miljat, Gary Wroblewski, Randy Butters, Jim Laganowski, and Charlie Grimm.

I'd also like to thank the *Journal Sentinel*'s Managing Editor, George Stanley, who encouraged me to begin writing a column of lake profiles called "Riepenhoff on Local Lakes." The idea was to visit lakes that you could reach in a day's trip from Milwaukee, write about my fishing experiences and the methods we used, and provide information about the fish species in each lake, fish stocking, management, special regulations, and public access.

This book is a collection of forty-four of those columns, covering fifty-five different lakes, written from 2000 to 2003. I've organized them into chapters by fish species. Some lakes offer good fishing for many different species. For those, I went with either the kind of fish we caught or the species for which the lake is best known, while including some cross references in the chapter introductions. Contour maps of each lake are included.

They show the locations of boat landings, and list the fish species present for each lake.

I'd like to give special thanks to my son, John, for his drawings of fish that begin each chapter.

This book is intended to help all anglers, from beginners to experts, to have more productive and enjoyable fishing experiences. Whether you want to hang a trophy bass or musky on your wall or you just want to spend a few quiet hours catching panfish with your kids, the information on these pages can help you reach your goal and make your dream come true.

NET

RESULTS

Bass

J. Riepenhoff

Bass

J. Riponhoft

I have a theory about why bass are the most pursued game fish in southern Wisconsin. It's not because they are abundant, with healthy populations thriving in most lakes. And it's not because they are relatively easy to catch, readily striking just about everything from live bait to spinners, top-waters, minnow imitations and plastics.

For me, the main reason for the attraction is pure and simple: Bass jump. Hook into a good-sized bass, feel its awesome power and watch as it explodes from the surface in a splashing, head-banging tail-dance and your adrenalin will start to pump. In that instant, frozen in time, you'll see the white of its belly, the red of its gills and the fire in its eyes.

That's when you'll understand what bass fishing is all about.

Largemouth bass are the most common bass in the southern part of the state.

In spring, bass move to the warmest water in the lake, typically the shallow bays.

Cast for them in the shady water of shoreline structure, including sunken logs, overhanging trees, docks and piers. They will readily take live bait, including a night crawler, leech or minnow, and a wide assortment of artificial lures, including top-waters, plastic worms, spinner baits, minnow imitations, and small plastic lures such as twister tails and tube jigs. One of my favorites is a pre-rigged plastic worm because it's so easy to use. Just attach the monofilament leader to a snap swivel tied to your line and start fishing.

Bass generally start to spawn in the shallows when the water temperature climbs above 60 degrees. They are extremely vulnerable when on their spawning beds and it's best to just leave them alone at this time.

In summer, bass can still be caught in shallow water using the same techniques, but you can also find them in deep water, near weed edges. A crank bait, a jig and pig, a Texas-rigged plastic worm or live bait presented in deep water, along the outside weed edge, can produce big fish. Also try casting spinner baits or twitching minnow baits over the weed flats, especially at dawn or dusk. If you are a fly fisherman, cast a popper or a wet fly in the same areas.

On heavily fished lakes with a lot of boat traffic, try fishing at night with a spinner bait, buzz bait, or any noisy surface lure or bait that rattles.

In fall, bass can be found just about anywhere, shallow or deep, near structure or weeds. The best clue is to look for green weeds, which give off oxygen and hold fish.

I caught my biggest largemouth bass, a five-pound, ten-ounce beauty, by dragging a night crawler along a deep weed line in fall.

I've profiled 14 great largemouth bass lakes in this chapter.

Smallmouth bass aren't as common in southern Wisconsin, but there are several lakes with good smallmouth populations. Smallmouth bass fight and jump just like largemouths, only they do it longer and harder.

Many of the same techniques that catch largemouths also work for smallmouth bass, but smallmouths are found in different habitats. They prefer rock reefs and sand bars to weed beds. I've had luck with night crawlers and leeches, plus minnow baits, tube jigs, twister tails and plastics that imitate crayfish.

Pine and Big Green lakes are profiled in this chapter. Other lakes that hold smallmouth bass include Oconomowoc, Okauchee, Geneva, Rock, the Nemahbins, Pewaukee, Nagawicka, Monona and Mendota, which are profiled in other chapters.

For a unique bass fishing experience, try Lake Columbia in Portage County, which is actually a power plant cooling reservoir that offers open-water largemouth and smallmouth bass fishing year-round. The lake has a carry-in-only boat launch and plenty of shore fishing access. Lake Columbia is the only Wisconsin lake with hybrid striped bass, a cross between white bass and ocean striped bass.

BIG CEDAR LAKE/WASHINGTON COUNTY

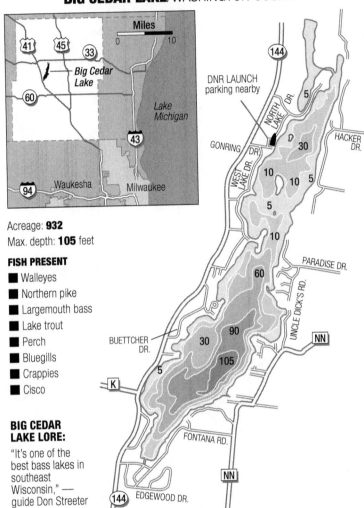

Acreage: **932**
Max. depth: **105** feet

FISH PRESENT

- ■ Walleyes
- ■ Northern pike
- ■ Largemouth bass
- ■ Lake trout
- ■ Perch
- ■ Bluegills
- ■ Crappies
- ■ Cisco

**BIG CEDAR
LAKE LORE:**

"It's one of the best bass lakes in southeast Wisconsin," — guide Don Streeter

Big Cedar Lake

WEST BEND—The plastic worm I was reeling over the top of a submerged weed bed was spiraling along in tight circles when, out from the dark vegetation, a largemouth bass suddenly appeared and inhaled it.

I worked the feisty fighter to boat-side, carefully removed the hook, released the bass and watched it swim back into the weeds and disappear.

"How many is that?" I asked Don Streeter, who was casting at the other end of the boat.

"About a dozen, I think," he replied.

The truth is, we'd both lost count. But that's easy to do when you're bass fishing on Big Cedar Lake.

"One of the Best"

"It's one of the best bass lakes in southeast Wisconsin," said Streeter, a guide who has fished the lake for 15 years.

John Nelson, fisheries biologist with the Department of Natural Resources (DNR) at Plymouth, agrees.

"The highlight of the lake, as far as sport fishing, is largemouth bass," Nelson said. "It's an action lake. It's not known for trophies, but 13- and 14-inch bass are common."

That's not to say that there are no trophy bass. "I've caught five-pounders," said Streeter, of Woodruff. "It's an action lake, but you also have the chance to get a trophy."

Big Cedar is a 932-acre clear-water lake with a maximum depth of 105 feet, located southeast of West Bend in Washington County. There are no boat rentals, but there is a public launch on Gonring Drive on the northwest end of the lake.

"The lake is split in two basins," Nelson said. "The south basin is deep and cold and the north basin is shallow and weedy."

Don Streeter shows off one of the largemouth bass he caught in Big Cedar Lake, which is known as one of the area's best largemouth bass lakes.

Since the water is very clear, fishing, in general, is best in the mornings and evenings, at night or on cloudy days. Like many southern Wisconsin lakes, the weekend boating pressure is best avoided, if possible.

But, Nelson said: "During the week, you can fish a lot of areas and not be disturbed."

In the past, the lake was also known for producing big northern pike but, in recent years, the pike population has declined to less than one fish per two acres.

As a result, Nelson said: "Starting in 2001, there is a one-fish daily bag and a 40-inch size limit for northern pike to maximize the opportunities for reproduction."

With good forage populations of suckers, perch, cisco and smelt, the lake still has tremendous potential to grow big northern pike.

"If we find the population is coming back and doing well, we could relax that regulation at some point," Nelson said.

Trout and Walleye Stocked

The DNR stocks about 93,000 walleye and 30,000 lake trout fingerlings every other year.

"The walleye population seems to be doing well," Nelson said. "Surveys show one and a half to two adult walleyes per acre."

The forage base also creates potential to put a real "wall hanger" walleye in the boat.

"We see a number of 12-pound walleyes in spring surveys," Nelson said. "One angler reported catching a 32-incher that weighed an estimated 15 pounds through the ice in February of 2001."

In the summer months, walleyes are caught on the rock humps, mud flats or submerged weed islands, mostly at night.

"It's primarily a night bite for walleyes," Nelson said. "Some of the best action is at one in the morning."

A good time to try for a trophy walleye is late fall. "In late November and early December, the cisco come on the rock reefs on the south end of the lake to spawn and the walleyes follow them," Nelson said.

The lake trout can be even more elusive.

"People catch them through the ice in the winter using cut bait in 75 to 90 feet of water, about a foot off the bottom," Nelson said. "In summer, some people catch them about 35 feet down at the thermocline."

Panfish are easier to locate.

"In the early spring, the crappies move into the shallow bay on the north end to spawn," Nelson said.

Bluegills can be found just about anywhere along the shoreline shallows in spring and early summer. Later in the summer, you can catch them by drifting over deep water about 15 feet down.

"The perch population seems to be picking up," Nelson said. "There are a few anglers that know where to find them. I'd guess they're fishing 25 feet down on a rock bar."

Streeter prefers to concentrate on the bass.

"You can use a variety of techniques," he said. "Work the shoreline structure with plastics, the flats with spinners or surface baits, or the deep weed line with crank baits or plastics. If one technique doesn't work, the next one will."

In late summer when the weeds are up, Streeter likes to work plastic frogs over the lily pads in Gilbert Lake, which is accessed through a channel on the north end. We've caught some big bass, up to about 18 inches long, using that method.

LAKE BEULAH/WALWORTH COUNTY

Acreage: **834**
Max. depth: **58** feet

FISH PRESENT

■ Walleyes
  (not common)
■ Northern pike
■ Largemouth bass
■ Panfish
■ Trout

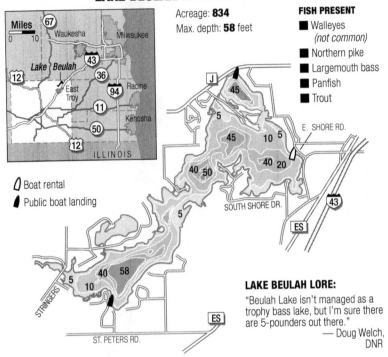

◖ Boat rental
◣ Public boat landing

LAKE BEULAH LORE:

"Beulah Lake isn't managed as a
trophy bass lake, but I'm sure there
are 5-pounders out there."
— Doug Welch,
DNR

Lake Beulah

EAST TROY—Through dark sunglasses, I could just make out the spot where the edge of a submerged weed bed met the deep water.

That's where I cast a long, black, plastic worm, rigged "weedless" on a jig, and let it drop. When I reeled in the slack and felt a sharp tug, I set the hook hard.

A moment later, a big largemouth bass splashed from the surface of the water in a frenzy of wild, head-banging gyrations.

It took a while to get things under control and lead the fish into the net in Gary Wroblewski's hands.

The bass was a good one. It bumped the ruler at close to 18 inches. I took a long last look, then let it go in the clear water of Lake Beulah.

If I had to pick my favorite largemouth bass lakes in southern Wisconsin, Lake Beulah would definitely make the short list.

I first fished the lake more than ten years ago with Wroblewski, a skilled angler with 25 years of experience on Lake Beulah.

Since then, we've managed to visit the lake a couple times a year and have had some very good days, including this trip, when we caught and released close to 40 bass, half of which were quality bass, ranging from about 14 to 18 inches long.

That would qualify as great bass action anywhere on earth. But, for southern Wisconsin, it was nothing short of spectacular.

Lake Beulah is an 834-acre lake with a maximum depth of 58 feet, located north of East Troy in Walworth County. It has good populations of bluegills, crappies and other panfish; some naturally reproducing northern pike; plus a few stocked walleyes.

But, as Wroblewski puts it: "The lake is dominated by largemouth bass."

The Town of East Troy operates a public boat launch on the southwest end, off Wilmer's Landing Road. Boat rentals are available at the Dockside Grog and Galley, on E. Shore Road off Highway ES on the east side of the lake.

According to Doug Welch, senior fisheries biologist with the Department of Natural Resources at Sturtevant, there is no annual stocking program for Lake Beulah.

Gary Wroblewski admires a healthy largemouth bass from Lake Beulah before releasing the big fish.

It isn't necessary.

Panfish, mostly bluegills and crappies, are naturally abundant. I recall one cool spring day a few years back when Wroblewski and I got into a nice mess of crappies.

There are northern pike. In winter, tip-up fishing for northerns is popular. "I've heard of 35- to 40-inch northerns caught through the ice," Welch said.

And in 1998, about 600 walleyes averaging 13 inches long were transferred from Delavan Lake to thin out a slow-growing walleye population in Delavan Lake and produce some additional fishing opportunities in Lake Beulah.

In addition, each spring the DNR stocks one thousand to two thousand 9- to 12-inch hatchery-raised brown trout to provide additional fishing opportunities. Most are caught in the first few weeks of the fishing season. But some may survive year to year, Welch said.

But Lake Beulah is best known among anglers for its largemouth bass. Welch called it "one of the best bass lakes in southern Wisconsin."

He credits special bass regulations, in effect on the lake since the early 1980s, that create a protected "slot" of bass from 12 to 16 inches long.

"You can keep fish under 12 inches and over 16 inches," Welch said. "The regulations were designed to protect spawning-age females from harvest, improve the size structure of bass and increase predation on bluegills.

"It's not really a trophy bass fishery. There are not a lot of bass over 18 inches. It's a quality fishery, where anglers get a lot of action and improved chances of getting a bass larger than 16 inches."

From my experience, the regulations are doing exactly what they were intended to do. Bass are abundant and the action can be fast and furious, as Wroblewski and I have found.

"The key to catching bass on Beulah is to remember that the bass are weed-oriented," said Wroblewski, of Eagle. "There is no defined weed line. The weeds are scattered throughout the lake, and all of them can hold good concentrations of bass."

As a result, Wroblewski said: "The bass can be in anything from two feet of water to 20 feet. And virtually any bass lure or method can work at any given time. It's a good lake to experiment with different techniques."

We launched Wroblewski's boat early one July morning and started the day casting poppers and other surface lures over the tops of the weeds on a weed flat.

An hour or so later when the action slowed, we switched to minnow baits, either twitching them over the weeds or running them in the open pockets or along the weed edges. Later, we switched to casting plastic worms along the deep weed edges.

"I like to rig a plastic worm on a quarter-ounce jig with a bait-holder hook and work it along the deep weeds," Wroblewski said. "This is a great technique for bigger bass."

That's true, but every technique we tried produced bass.

On other trips, we've also had luck casting spinner baits along the weed edges or over the tops of the weeds in less than ten feet of water, especially at night.

Although several of our bass exceeded the 16-inch protected slot, Wroblewski and I released everything we caught.

"The majority of fishermen release the bass they catch on Beulah," Wroblewski said. "That keeps the population healthy and the bigger fish in the lake."

GENESEE LAKES/WAUKESHA COUNTY

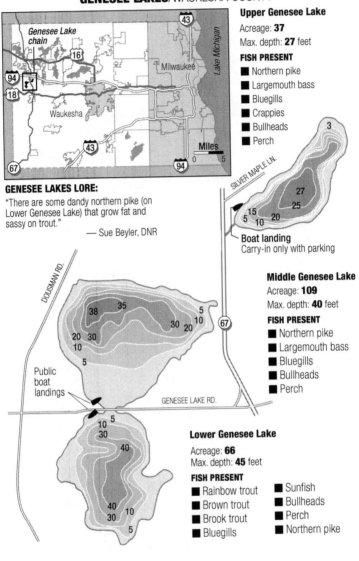

Genesee Lake chain

Milwaukee

Waukesha

Lake Michigan

Miles
0   5

Upper Genesee Lake

Acreage: **37**
Max. depth: **27** feet

FISH PRESENT
■ Northern pike
■ Largemouth bass
■ Bluegills
■ Crappies
■ Bullheads
■ Perch

GENESEE LAKES LORE:
"There are some dandy northern pike (on Lower Genesee Lake) that grow fat and sassy on trout."
— Sue Beyler, DNR

Boat landing
Carry-in only with parking

SILVER MAPLE LN.

DOUSMAN RD.

Public boat landings

GENESEE LAKE RD.

Middle Genesee Lake

Acreage: **109**
Max. depth: **40** feet

FISH PRESENT
■ Northern pike
■ Largemouth bass
■ Bluegills
■ Bullheads
■ Perch

Lower Genesee Lake

Acreage: **66**
Max. depth: **45** feet

FISH PRESENT
■ Rainbow trout   ■ Sunfish
■ Brown trout   ■ Bullheads
■ Brook trout   ■ Perch
■ Bluegills   ■ Northern pike

Upper, Middle and Lower Genesee Lakes

DOUSMAN—As we used a home-made bicycle-wheel dolly to roll Bill Stauber's 12-foot aluminum fishing boat down a tree-lined path that leads to Upper Genesee Lake, I could tell we were in for a different kind of fishing experience.

Access to Upper Genesee is "carry-in" only, which limits it to small boats or canoes, and there are just five free parking spots. A Town of Summit regulation also prohibits the use of motors on this quiet little 37-acre lake with a maximum depth of 27 feet.

All that is fine with Stauber, my brother-in-law, who has fished this lake for close to ten years.

"I go for the setting as much as the fishing," Stauber told me. "It almost has the feel of a wilderness lake. The only development you see is a handful of home sites."

The path goes on for a hundred yards or so and leads to a mucky, unimproved launch site, so rubber boots or bare feet are probably a good idea.

The lake's fishing structure is relatively simple.

"It's basically a bowl," said Sue Beyler, senior Department of Natural Resources fisheries biologist for Waukesha County. "It has some nice steep drop-offs on the northeast side with shallow bays at either end."

Our boat was the only one on the lake that September afternoon. So it was quiet and peaceful as we rowed along, working the shoreline structure with a plastic worm or live bait—either a fathead minnow or a piece of night crawler—suspended beneath a bobber.

"You can fish it in a few hours," said Stauber, of Wauwatosa. "The fishing action is usually pretty fair."

In the 1990s, the DNR stocked 150 northern pike a year to augment a natural population, but there has been no stocking of any species in recent years.

"We don't stock lakes that don't need it," Beyler said.

Bill Stauber prepares to launch his boat at the carry-in landing of Upper Genesee Lake in Waukesha County.

The last survey, done in 1980, found largemouth bass up to 20 inches, northerns up to 19 inches, bluegills up to eight inches, perch up to 11 inches, plus crappies and bullheads.

"A Healthy Lake"

"There's definitely the potential for big bass," Beyler said. "There's plenty of bluegills, plenty of minnows. It's a nice healthy lake."

We enjoyed the scenery as we fished the tree-lined shores. We caught and released a half-dozen bass, up to about 13 inches, plus a dozen or more bluegills up to about 7 inches, before a thunderstorm cut our trip a little short.

"I think limiting the access to five boats is good for the lake," Stauber said afterward. "It limits the amount of fishing pressure."

If you have a bigger boat, or the carry-in idea doesn't appeal to you, consider Middle Genesee Lake to the west, which has a free launch on the south side of Genesee Lake Road.

Middle Genesee is a 109-acre, clear-water lake with a maximum depth of 40 feet. The DNR stocks 550 six-inch northern pike every year to bolster a natural population. In addition, a 1998 survey found largemouth bass up to 17 inches and bluegills up to ten inches, plus perch and bullheads.

"It has nice panfish," Beyler said. "I was impressed with the size of the bluegills."

Middle Genesee is, basically, another bowl, but there is some structure.

"It has a sandy bottom, weed beds near the outlet on the north shore, and deep areas along the north shore," Beyler said. "The south side is a big shallow flat."

Across the street from the launch, on the north side of Genesee Lake Road, is the boat landing for the third lake on this chain, Lower Genesee Lake. The Lower and Middle Genesee launches share a free parking lot about a block to the west, which also provides a couple hundred feet of shore fishing access. There are no boat rentals on any of the three lakes.

"That launch leaves a lot to be desired," Beyler said of the unimproved, sand boat landing on Lower Genesee. "The water is shallow by the ramp. You shouldn't plan on taking anything too big."

When I paid an opening day visit to Lower Genesee Lake a few years back, that sandy launch convinced us to use a canoe. We fished for trout and caught a bunch of them, mostly on small spinners, or minnows suspended beneath slip bobbers.

Lower Genesee is a 66-acre lake with a maximum depth of 45 feet. The DNR stocks three thousand brown trout, three thousand rainbows, and two thousand brook trout each year for put-and-take fishing.

Strictly Recreation

"This is strictly to provide recreation," Beyler said. "We don't expect them to reproduce."

Most of the trout, which average about ten inches long, are caught within the first two or three weeks of the season, Beyler said, but some are caught through the ice each winter and a few survive to the following spring.

"Once in a while we get a report of someone catching a 14- or 15-incher," Beyler said. "We know that fish wasn't stocked that year."

The lake also has natural fish populations. A 1998 survey found bass up to 13 inches, bluegills up to nine inches, plus perch, sunfish, bullheads and northern pike.

In fact, Lower Genesee has a reputation for producing some monster northerns.

"There are some dandy northern pike that grow fat and sassy on those trout," Beyler explained.

LAKE KEESUS/WAUKESHA COUNTY

Acreage: **237**
Max. depth: **42** feet

FISH PRESENT

■ Largemouth bass
■ Northern pike
■ Walleyes
■ Bluegills
■ Perch
■ Crappies
■ Sunfish

LAKE KEESUS LORE:

"It's a very nice fishery. There's such a good balance between the bass and the bluegills."

— Sue Beyler,
  DNR

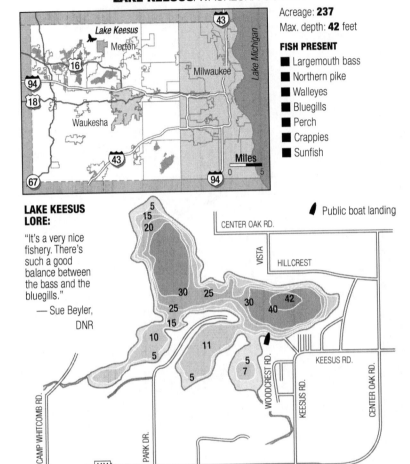

Lake Keesus

MERTON—The first thing that struck me about Lake Keesus was all the panfish that were swarming around the shoreline weeds right at the boat landing.

I watched through Polaroid sun glasses as bluegills, mostly, but also some perch and even a few small bass darted back and forth.

It was an encouraging sign for Don Streeter and me as we set out one August morning for what turned out to be a great day of largemouth bass fishing.

"That's one of the nicest bass and bluegill lakes that I've seen," Sue Beyler said of Lake Keesus. "It's a very nice fishery. There's such a good balance between the bass and the bluegills."

At 237 acres, Lake Keesus has a maximum depth of 42 feet. The lake management district operates the only boat launch ($6) off Woodcrest Road on the southeast side of the lake. There are no boat rentals.

This north-central Waukesha County lake has natural populations of largemouth bass, northern pike, bluegills, crappies, perch and sunfish.

A DNR fish shocking survey conducted in 2001 showed bass ranging from 6 to 20 inches long, with an average length of about 12 inches.

"It has a well balanced bass population with good reproduction, good growth and bass of various sizes," Beyler said. "Sixteen- and seventeen-inch bass were common when we shocked. With lots of panfish, I would say there is plenty of food and very good growth potential."

The survey also showed northern pike from 9 to 29 inches long, with an average length of 20 inches; and bluegills from three to ten inches long, with an average length of 6½ inches.

The lake also has natural populations of perch, crappies and sunfish.

"Bluegills are the most predominant panfish," Beyler said. "That lake has quantity, but it also has quality panfish. You have big bass that are keeping the bluegills in check. And there is plenty of spawning habitat, so there's no danger of them being over-grazed."

In addition, the DNR has been stocking walleyes since 1999.

"The lake association had started stocking walleyes a few years back and they wanted us to continue," Beyler said.

Don Streeter lowers a good-sized bass to the water as he's about to release it back into Lake Keesus in north-central Waukesha County.

The DNR stocked 23,000 fingerling walleyes in 1999 and 2001.

"In fall of 2001, we shocked and found 35 walleyes from about six to nine inches long," Beyler said. "That told us that they did well, they 'took,' so we're going to continue stocking them every other year."

Lake Keesus is made up of a series of bays that offer an impressive variety of good structure.

Walleyes in Deep

"It has a lot of deep water," Beyler said. "It drops off sharply along the east and north shorelines. It's really steep. That deep water, along the break lines, is where people are going to find the walleyes."

Streeter and I were after bass. We used an electric trolling motor to work our way around the lake, using medium-action spinning gear to throw plastic baits, either night crawlers or crawfish. We concentrated on shoreline structure, including that inside weed line, some shallow lily-pad bays, or piers and docked pontoon boats where we caught and released lots of bass.

We saw panfish under almost every pier, especially on the northeast side. So many of them chased out from the dark water to nip at the plastic worms that I made a mental note to return some day to fish for bluegills.

This time, though, we kept busy enough catching bass. In a few hours of fishing, we caught and released more than dozen.

Streeter, a guide and bass tournament angler, was impressed.

"We caught a variety of different-sized bass," Streeter said. "They weren't all carbon copies. We caught fish from different years, including some decent ones that were 15, 16, 17 inches long."

Big Bass Hits

And then there was the big fish of the day.

It hit after I made a long a cast and started reeling a plastic worm as close as I could run it along the inside weed line.

I felt some resistance and set the hook.

The bass didn't jump or even make so much as a splash. Instead, it began a series of incredibly powerful underwater runs for the deep water.

It took almost five minutes before I was able to bring the heavy, dark-colored bass to boat-side. I unhooked the big bass and, before I let it go, held it up against an 18-inch ruler that Streeter keeps in the boat.

This one was at least a full inch longer.

SILVER LAKE/WAUKESHA COUNTY

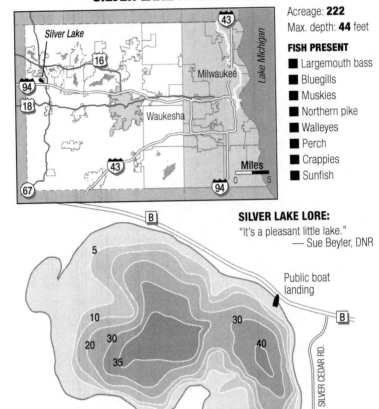

Acreage: **222**
Max. depth: **44** feet

FISH PRESENT
- Largemouth bass
- Bluegills
- Muskies
- Northern pike
- Walleyes
- Perch
- Crappies
- Sunfish

SILVER LAKE LORE:
"It's a pleasant little lake."
— Sue Beyler, DNR

Public boat landing

Silver Lake

Milwaukee

Waukesha

Lake Michigan

Miles
0   5

SILVER CEDAR RD.

Silver Lake

OCONOMOWOC—"Pleasant" is a word that comes to mind when I think about Silver Lake in western Waukesha County "Bass" and "bluegills" are two more.

At 222 acres with a maximum depth of 44 feet, Silver Lake is a clear, pretty lake that's small enough to fish your way around in a few hours. When I've fished it, the boat traffic hasn't been too bad, compared with the larger lakes in the neighborhood.

"The two primary species sought by anglers are largemouth bass and bluegills," said the DNR's Sue Beyler.

A DNR survey conducted in the mid-1990s showed bluegills up to $8\frac{1}{2}$ inches long, with 58 percent of the bluegills sampled six inches or longer.

"That indicates a well-balanced bluegill population," Beyler said. "I was impressed by the fact that we saw nice catching size bluegills."

While largemouth bass are abundant, the survey didn't show many bass over the legal limit of 14 inches.

"Most were in the 10- to $13\frac{1}{2}$-inch class," Beyler said. "It looks like they may be a little behind in their growth rates."

Also, Beyler said, some of the larger bass may have been "cropped off" over the years.

Silver Lake also has a small but naturally reproducing population of northern pike "in the 18- to 26-inch range," Beyler said, plus a few perch, sunfish and crappies.

"Bluegills are definitely the dominant panfish," she said.

In addition, the DNR has stocked about 11,000 two- to three-inch walleye fingerlings every other year since the mid-1990s, at the request of local property owners.

The DNR operates a free public boat launch on Highway B on the north side of the lake.

"The launch is right off the road, and you have to cross the road to get to the parking lot," Beyler said. "It's kind of hazardous."

There are no boat rentals.

29

A largemouth bass is taken at Silver Lake with a minnow bait.

Nooks and Crannies

The lake has some interesting features, including a bull rush island on the east end and a shallow marsh-lined kettle on the west end.

"That marsh acts as a refuge because it's shallow and difficult for boats to get in there," Beyler said. "It's definitely a spawning area for bass, bluegills and northern pike."

Don Streeter and I have fished Silver Lake for both bass and bluegills several times. In general, we work the piers and shoreline structure for bass, and the submerged weeds for bluegills.

This time, after launching Streeter's boat one May evening, we motored over to the bull rush island, where there is a steep drop-off. We worked our way around, using medium-action spinning gear to cast a plastic worm or a minnow bait. We caught and released a couple bass in the 12-inch range before moving on.

As we used an electric trolling motor to move quietly along the shallows, we observed several male bass making and guarding their spawning beds—irregularly shaped patches of gravel lake bottom that they brushed clear with their fins. When the water temperature warms, the female bass will move in and drop their eggs.

It's a fascinating process. But, as Streeter said: "It's best to leave spawning bass alone to ensure future fishing."

We decided to move over to a windswept bay on the south shore, where we anchored in about five feet of water and used ultralight spinning gear to cast live bait—either a wax worm or a piece of night crawler suspended beneath a bobber—into the shoreline shallows.

Small Yields

We had steady action catching bluegills, but they were all pretty small, so we let them go.

"In spring, the small panfish move into the shallows first," Streeter explained.

So we pulled the anchor and continued our way around the lake, casting into the shallows, the drop-offs and the shoreline structure, picking up a few more bass, here and there.

"It's one of those nice clear lakes that you can spend a half day fishing the whole thing and enjoying yourself," Streeter said afterward. "I wouldn't go there looking for a trophy, but there are three- and four-pound bass in the lake."

There's nothing wrong with catching a few of those, right?

MOOSE LAKE/WAUKESHA COUNTY

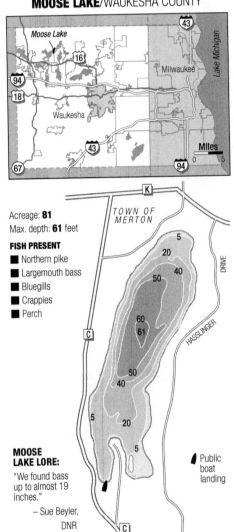

Acreage: **81**
Max. depth: **61** feet

FISH PRESENT

■ Northern pike
■ Largemouth bass
■ Bluegills
■ Crappies
■ Perch

**MOOSE
LAKE LORE:**

"We found bass
up to almost 19
inches."

— Sue Beyler,
DNR

Public
boat
landing

Moose Lake

CHENEQUA—After a long cast into the clear, shoreline shallows of Moose Lake, I felt a tug on the line, set the hook and saw a healthy largemouth bass explode from the water and splash skyward.

The fish jumped two more times before I could bring it to the boat, lip it, unhook the plastic worm and watch it swim off. It was the kind of largemouth bass action Don Streeter and I had hoped for the moment we laid eyes on Moose Lake. Neither of us had fished it before making two trips.

"I like this lake," said Streeter, a guide and bass tournament angler. "The clear water and the natural structure make it seem like an 'up north' lake."

Moose Lake is an 81-acre lake with a maximum depth of 61 feet. It has plenty of weeds, rocks, steep drop-offs and other structure that you look for in a good bass lake.

According to Sue Beyler, the state has not stocked fish in Moose Lake since 1976, because of insufficient public access.

That might change soon.

The DNR has purchased 2.3 acres on the south end of the lake for development of a public access. Plans call for an improved launch, a public fishing pier, and parking for four vehicles with trailers, plus two cars and one vehicle and trailer for the disabled.

"Once we get that public pier in, it's going to be one of the nicest ones in the region," Beyler said. "There is deep, clear water with plenty of plants."

In the Meantime

Meanwhile, an existing launch, with parking for four cars with trailers, remains open. The launch is located at the end of a gravel road off Highway C on the south end of the lake. There is no charge. There are no boat rentals.

Historically, the DNR stocked Moose Lake with rainbow and brown trout from 1951 to 1976.

Don Streeter unhooks a largemouth bass he caught during an outing on Waukesha County's Moose Lake.

"My goal is to resume stocking rainbow trout," Beyler said, although the earliest that could happen would probably be 2006. "It's deep, it's clear, it's cold and it can hold trout, year to year."

During fyke net and boom-shock surveys, DNR crews did not find any holdover trout, and Beyler doubts that there are any left in the lake.

The surveys found lots of largemouth bass, mostly in the 13- to 15-inch range, but some bigger.

"We found bass up to almost 19 inches," Beyler said. "My feeling is there are a lot of bass out there from what we observed."

Of the bass sampled, she said: "The number of quality fish—12 inches or longer—was 75 percent. There is excellent size structure for largemouth bass."

The crews found lots of northern pike in the 16- to 22-inch range, plus a 30- and a 32-incher. In addition, Beyler said: "We saw a big northern—it looked like it could have been close to 40 inches."

They also found naturally reproducing populations of bluegills up to eight inches, crappies in the ten-inch range, plus perch, rock bass and sunfish.

Streeter and I fished the shoreline structure all the way around the lake on two afternoons. The second time we were joined by Chuck Smrcina, of Menomonee Falls, who fished in a separate boat.

We used medium-action spinning gear to cast either a plastic worm, a minnow bait or a piece of night crawler on a plain hook with a split-shot. We worked the sunken trees, overhanging willows, inside weed line, gravel flats, drop-offs, piers and anything else that looked as if it might hold fish.

We observed some bass still making spawning beds in the shallows, but they were in very skittish moods. Others seemed to be staging in slightly deeper water.

Tread Lightly

"With the clear water, you have to use light line and make long casts," said Streeter. "You have to be extremely quiet. If a bass sees the boat, you won't catch it."

With the clear water, this might be a good lake to fish at night or on an overcast day.

Even in the afternoon sun, we managed to catch and release about a half-dozen bass—including a couple that reached the "keeper" size of 14 inches—on each trip, plus a few small northerns, bluegills and rock bass.

"I'd like to come back and fish this lake later in the summer," Streeter said. "It has a lot of structure that you know is going to hold fish."

WHITEWATER/RICE LAKES/WALWORTH COUNTY

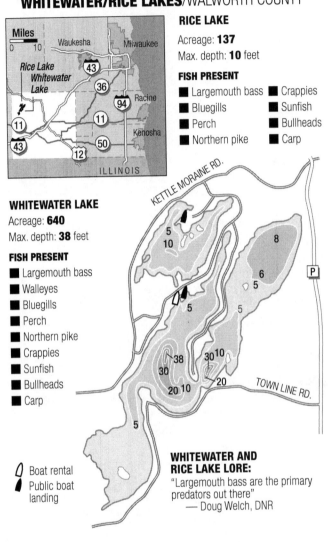

RICE LAKE

Acreage: **137**
Max. depth: **10** feet

FISH PRESENT

- Largemouth bass
- Bluegills
- Perch
- Northern pike
- Crappies
- Sunfish
- Bullheads
- Carp

WHITEWATER LAKE

Acreage: **640**
Max. depth: **38** feet

FISH PRESENT

- Largemouth bass
- Walleyes
- Bluegills
- Perch
- Northern pike
- Crappies
- Sunfish
- Bullheads
- Carp

Boat rental

Public boat
landing

WHITEWATER AND RICE LAKE LORE:

"Largemouth bass are the primary
predators out there"
— Doug Welch, DNR

Whitewater and Rice Lakes

WHITEWATER—A park setting, plenty of shore-fishing access, a good variety of fish and the chance for a trophy bass.

If any of those elements grab you, you might want to check out Whitewater and Rice lakes. Tucked in a corner of the Kettle Moraine State Forest in the northwest part of Walworth County, this pretty pair of lakes can provide some excellent fishing, especially for largemouth bass.

Whitewater Lake is the bigger of the two, at 640 acres with a maximum depth of 38 feet. Rice Lake, to the northwest, is 137 acres with a maximum depth of just ten feet.

Both lakes have healthy, naturally reproducing populations of bass.

"Largemouth bass are the primary predator out there," said Doug Welch with the DNR.

Whitewater Lake, in particular, is known for bigger-than-average bass.

"That lake grows bass up to 22 or 24 inches," Welch said. "So we're talking five or six pounders."

The DNR stocks Whitewater Lake with about 30,000 to 60,000 walleye fingerlings and about 1,000 to 2,000 eight-inch northerns every other year, Welch said. The DNR also transferred some adult walleyes from Delavan Lake in 1997 in an attempt to get better growth rates on Delavan.

Rice Lake has the same fish species as Whitewater, except for walleyes. The DNR periodically stocks northern pike in Rice Lake. This spring, the state stocked 400 northern pike, plus 3,500 largemouth bass fingerlings because of a partial winter kill the previous winter, Welch said.

Panfish Aplenty

Both lakes have natural populations of panfish—bluegills, crappies and perch.

A fish survey of Rice Lake this spring found bass up to 18 inches long, crappies up to nine inches and bluegills up to seven inches.

Since both lakes are located in the Whitewater Lake State Recreation Area, a state park sticker, or a daily admission fee of $5, is required. There is no additional cost to launch your boat on either lake.

Tim Komar pulls the hook from a 16-inch largemouth bass taken from Whitewater Lake.

Parkside Marina, at N7660 State Park Road, rents fishing boats, canoes and pontoon boats for Whitewater Lake. A rowboat costs $47 a day and a boat and motor costs $68. There are no boat rentals on Rice Lake.

Both lakes have good shore fishing access.

"Rice Lake has shore access all the way around, except for a few small portions," Welch said. "Ninety percent of the shoreline is state owned."

On Whitewater Lake, there is shore access on state land near the launch on the northwest end.

Whitewater Lake is made up of a series of lobes that almost seem like separate lakes. Its distinguishing characteristics include two floating bog islands and a thick crop of Eurasian milfoil.

"The lake management district has a milfoil harvest program," Welch said. "But it's like cutting a lawn—it keeps coming back."

Rice Lake is connected to Whitewater by a narrow outlet on the northwest end of Whitewater Lake, and the habitat and water quality of both lakes are similar.

"What works on one lake usually works on the other," said Tim Komar, a guide and tournament angler who has fished the lakes for about seven years. "Rice is smaller and more sheltered from the wind."

Both lakes have dark-stained water.

"That tends to keep the fish shallow," Komar explained. "You can get closer to the fish without spooking them than you can on a clear lake."

I met up with Komar, of Elkhorn, on a sunny but cool June morning when the water temperature was 57 degrees, a two-degree drop from the day before.

We fished Whitewater in the morning and Rice in the afternoon, using basically the same techniques. We used both spinning and bait-casting gear to work plastic worms, plastic "Guido bug" crawfish, or small crank baits between the inside weed line and shore. We also pitched the plastic baits into the tangled brush of the bog and island shorelines.

Slow Action

We caught bass, but the action was slower than we expected.

"Usually, it's pretty easy to catch a limit of 14- to 15-inch fish," Komar said. "The fish are generally more aggressive."

Komar blamed the slow bite on a warm spell, followed by cooler weather, which may have confused or delayed the bass spawn.

Even so, we managed to catch and release more than a half dozen bass— a 16-incher, a 14-incher and several in the 12-inch range.

"Catch and release is important on these lakes," Komar said, "especially in spring when the bass are spawning."

KETTLE MORAINE LAKES/NORTHERN UNIT

Lake Winnebago

SHEBOYGAN COUNTY

FOND DU LAC COUNTY

MILWAUKEE COUNTY

Lake Michigan

LAKE LORE:

"These are quiet lakes where you can get away from the crowd. All of them are best fished from a canoe or small row boat." — John Nelson, DNR

◢ Public boat landing

FISH PRESENT

CROOKED LAKE
- ■ Largemouth bass
- ■ Northern pike
- ■ Bluegills
- ■ Crappies

LAKE SEVEN
- ■ Largemouth bass
- ■ Northern pike
- ■ Bluegills
- ■ Perch

FOREST LAKE
- ■ Largemouth bass
- ■ Northern pike
- ■ Walleyes
- ■ Bluegills

MAUTHE LAKE
- ■ Largemouth bass
- ■ Northern pike
- ■ Walleyes
- ■ Bluegills
- ■ Crappies

AUBURN LAKE
- ■ Largemouth bass
- ■ Northern pike
- ■ Walleyes
- ■ Yellow bass

S.E. WISCONSIN AREA ▲   **DETAIL** ▼

KETTLE MORAINE FOREST
(NORTHERN UNIT)

DAVIDSON RD.

W

Auburn Lake Creek

67

HAUSHALTER RD.

G

River E. Branch

Crooked Lake

RD.

SS

Lake Seven

N. MAPLE TREE RD.

Mauthe Lake

Forest Lake

Auburn Lake

FOREST VIEW RD.

TOWER DR.

45

G

Milwaukee

GGG

S

Mile

0   3/4

Crooked, Seven, Forest, Mauthe and Auburn Lakes

NEW PROSPECT—If you're looking for an "Up North" fishing experience but don't have time to make the drive from down south, here's a little tip.

Tucked in a corner of the Northern Unit of the Kettle Moraine State Forest, straddling the Fond du Lac–Sheboygan county line, there is a cluster of five beautiful little lakes where you can launch a small boat, get away from it all and probably catch a few largemouth bass in the process.

The lakes—Crooked, Seven, Forest, Mauthe and Auburn—are each about a hundred acres or less, and are located about an hour's drive from Milwaukee.

"These lakes have the atmosphere of the north woods," Jim Laganowski said as we drove along the tree-lined access road to the Crooked Lake boat landing. "You can paddle your way around any of them in a few hours," although motors are permitted.

For people like Laganowski, of Franklin, who has fished these lakes for years, the lakes offer tranquility, a feeling of remoteness and the opportunity for a quality fishing experience.

"These are quiet lakes where you can get away from the crowd," said John Nelson of the DNR. "All of them are best fished from a canoe or small rowboat. There's a lot of natural, undeveloped shoreline with downed trees."

The tangled branches of those sunken trees offer perfect places for bass to hide. Although there are other fish present, most anglers concentrate on largemouth bass, Nelson said.

Because the lakes are small, Nelson encourages catch and release for bass. "It wouldn't take much to over-fish these populations," he said.

Laganowski and I started our June day on Crooked Lake, a 91-acre lake with a maximum depth of 32 feet and lots of lily pads and other aquatic vegetation. The access road to the launch is north of Highway SS and west of Maple Tree Road.

Anglers cast in peace and quiet near the tree-lined shore on Auburn Lake, which features largemouth bass, northern pike, bluegills and yellow bass.

Good-sized Bass

"We did a survey in spring of 2000," Nelson said. "We didn't see a lot of bass, but the ones we saw were good size."

Laganowski and I caught and released a few bass by casting plastic worms along the weed edges. The biggest was almost 16 inches long.

Other species include northern pike, crappies and bluegills. Boat rentals are available at Hoeft's and Four Seasons resorts on the lake.

If you're looking for an "action lake," Nelson recommends Lake Seven, which is 27 acres with a maximum depth of 25 feet. There is a boat launch off Maple Tree Road, south of Highway SS.

"That lake has an unbelievable population of bass, as far as numbers," Nelson said. "There are mostly 10- to 12-inch fish. But we've had nights when we shocked several hundred in one trip around the lake." The lake also has some bluegills, northern pike and perch.

Forest Lake, which is 51 acres with a maximum depth of 32 feet, has special regulations that allow catch-and-release fishing only for bass, walleyes and northern pike.

There is a carry-in launch off Highway GGG, south of Highway SS. The path to the launch is about 50 yards down a steep hill, so you might want to use a light canoe or a float tube.

"The lake had a history of stunted panfish, mostly bluegills," Nelson said. "The special regulations try to keep as many predators as possible in the lake to improve the heath of the bluegill population."

As a side effect, he said: "There are probably some trophy bass in there."

Mauthe and Auburn lakes are located in "fee areas," where a state forest sticker is required. For state residents, the cost is $5 a day or $18 for an annual sticker.

Parkview General Store, located outside the entrance to the Mauthe Lake Recreational Area on Highway GGG, rents rowboats, canoes, kayaks and paddleboats on Mauthe Lake, and rowboats on Forest, Auburn and Lake Seven.

Good Bass Lake

Mauthe Lake is 78 acres with a maximum depth of 23 feet. The public launch is located off Highway GGG, south of Highway SS.

"Mauthe is a very good bass lake," Nelson said. "There is a distinct weed break in about 12 feet of water."

That weed edge is a good place to catch bass. Other species are northern pike, walleyes, bluegills and crappies.

Laganowski and I finished our day on Auburn Lake, which, including a south bay that some call "Little Auburn Lake," is 107 acres with a maximum depth of 29 feet. The boat landing is located south of Highway SS and west of Highway G, across from the entrance to the state forest headquarters.

Again, we cast plastic worms along the weed edges, and had action with a few more bass. There was just one other boat on the tree-lined lake.

In addition to largemouth bass, the lake has northern pike, bluegills and yellow bass—a species similar in appearance to white bass but smaller.

The DNR also stocks brook trout in Lake Fifteen Creek, a feeder creek to the north, and Nelson said: "I'm sure a few of those trout may get down to the lake."

Laganowski enjoys the quality fishing that these lakes offer.

"They're so close together," he said. "If the fish aren't biting on one lake, you have the opportunity to move to another one."

GOLDEN LAKE/WAUKESHA COUNTY

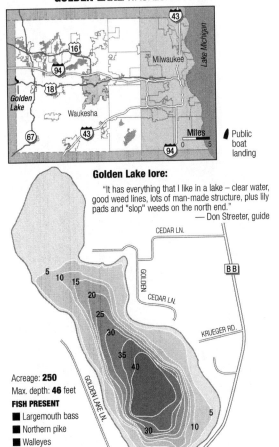

Golden Lake lore:

"It has everything that I like in a lake – clear water, good weed lines, lots of man-made structure, plus lily pads and "slop" weeds on the north end."
— Don Streeter, guide

Public boat landing

CEDAR LN.

GOLDEN

CEDAR LN.

KRUEGER RD.

B B

GOLDEN LAKE LN.

Acreage: **250**
Max. depth: **46** feet

FISH PRESENT

- Largemouth bass
- Northern pike
- Walleyes
- Crappies
- Bluegills
- Perch

To Waukesha

Golden Lake

SULLIVAN—I was casting a pre-rigged, three-hook plastic worm and slowly working it back over the top of a submerged weed bed on the west side of Golden Lake when something substantial hit it hard.

"I've got one," I bragged to Don Streeter, who was casting and reeling at the other end of the boat.

Streeter replied: "So do I."

Our doubleheader was on!

It took several minutes of jumping, splashing and reeling, but we finally managed to get things under control. When we did, we had a nice pair of largemouth bass in the boat.

After a picture or two, we let them go and watched them swim away.

This was my introduction to Golden Lake, a pretty, clear-water lake that straddles the Waukesha-Jefferson county line. Streeter had fished Golden Lake just one time before, for crappies many years ago.

Even so, we had no trouble finding some pretty good bass action one recent afternoon in June.

Good Fishing All Around

Golden Lake is a clear, spring-fed, 250-acre lake with a maximum depth of 46 feet. There are no boat rentals, but the DNR operates a free boat launch off Highway 18, and there is also some public land on the north end.

"I hesitate to call it shore access because it's so marshy," said Sue Beyler of the DNR. "But in the winter, ice fishing anglers can access the lake off of Golden Lake Park Road on the north."

The marsh on the north end also provides some natural, undeveloped shoreline, which can be hard to find these days on a southern Wisconsin lake.

The DNR stocks 12,500 walleye fingerlings every other year. In addition, there are naturally reproducing populations of largemouth bass, northern pike, bluegills, crappies, perch and sunfish.

Crappie fishing can be good, especially in the spring, and northern pike tend to grow relatively big.

"It's not uncommon to catch them 30 inches or longer," Beyler said.

Don Streeter releases a largemouth bass on Golden Lake in Sullivan.

Walleye Action Spotty

The walleye fishing can also be good, "on and off," she said. The last angler's creel survey, done in the early 1990s, showed that people were catching a fair number of walleyes at that time.

Even so, Beyler said: "It's primarily a bass lake. Bass are still the number one game fish on the lake."

That's what we were after when we launched Streeter's boat at the public landing on a warm and hazy afternoon.

I should offer a word of caution about the boat landing. The launch is on the north side of Highway 18 and the parking lot is in the south side. You have to drive across a busy highway to park, and visibility is limited. So take your time and be careful.

We used medium-action spinning and bait casting gear to throw a variety of lures as we worked our way around the lake, using an electric trolling motor.

We used floating Rapalas, spinner baits, plastic frogs, panfish grubs and those deadly pre-rigged plastic worms, and caught fish on just about everything we threw.

Bass in Varied Waters

We found both bass and bluegills in the shallow water, relating to piers and other shoreline structure. And we found more bass along the inside weed line, on the weed flats and in the thick "slop" weeds along the north end. In all, we must have caught and released about 15 bass, ranging from about 12 to 17 inches long, including four or five longer than the legal limit of 14 inches.

We also caught one northern, maybe 25 or 26 inches long, in the thick weeds on a "weedless" rubber frog.

"This is not the kind of lake where you have to concentrate on certain spots," Streeter said. "You can find fish all over the lake. You can fish deep or you can fish shallow. And it's laid out so you can get out of the wind if you have to."

The lake was also relatively quiet. Maybe its small size keeps the boat traffic down.

"It has everything that I like in a lake—clear water, good weed lines, lots of man-made structure, plus lily pads and 'slop' weeds on the north end," Streeter said. "I'll definitely be back to fish this lake again."

My sentiments, exactly.

LOWER SPRING LAKE/JEFFERSON COUNTY

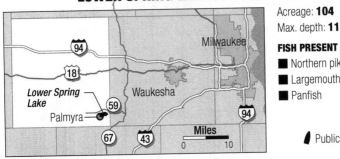

Acreage: **104**
Max. depth: **11** feet

FISH PRESENT
- Northern pike
- Largemouth bass
- Panfish

◢ Public boat launch

LOWER SPRING LAKE LORE:

"We've found bass up to 18 1/2 inches, but I'm sure there are bigger ones in the lake."
— Don Bush, DNR

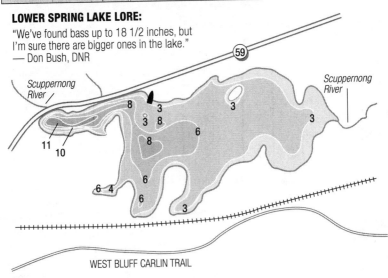

WEST BLUFF CARLIN TRAIL

Lower Spring Lake

PALMYRA—If at first you don't succeed, switch lures and try again.
That, more or less, was the lesson we came away with after a couple of encounters with Lower Spring Lake in Jefferson County.

Gary Wroblewski, Larry Awe of Wauwatosa, and I made our first trip to Lower Spring one June morning in search of largemouth bass. None of us had fished the lake before.

Lower Spring Lake is a shallow, 104-acre lake with a maximum depth of 11 feet. It is actually an impoundment created more than a hundred years ago by a dam on the Scuppernong River.

"The 11-foot area is probably all contained in a small hole next to the dam," said Don Bush, regional fisheries supervisor with the Department of Natural Resources in Janesville. "Most of the rest of the lake is about three feet deep."

Weeds Taking Over

The shallow water and a dirt-ramp public boat launch, located off Highway 59 on the north side of the lake, make a relatively small boat and outboard your best bet. There are no boat rentals.

Excessive weed growth is another limiting factor that can make boating difficult, especially on the east end and in the south bays.

"It has a lot of vegetation problems with both coontail and milfoil," Bush said. "The lake district tries to keep the weeds down, but it's a losing battle sometimes."

Because of the weed problem, boat access for anglers is best in spring, before the weeds grow, and in fall, after they start to die off.

But those weeds hold a lot of fish.

The DNR stocks about 200 five-inch northern pike fingerlings each year to supplement a natural population of northerns.

Beyond that, the lake has healthy, self-sustaining populations of largemouth bass, bluegills and pumpkinseeds, plus some sunfish, bullheads and an occasional grass pickerel, a small cousin to the northern pike.

There is plenty of access for shore anglers along Highway 59.

Gary Wroblewski removes the hook from a largemouth bass during his trip at Lower Spring Lake.

"It's a great place to take the kids and catch some panfish," Bush said. "The pumpkinseeds would be right up near shore in spring and early summer."

A fish-shocking survey in spring of 2001 showed lots of bluegills and pumpkinseeds, plus an excellent population of largemouth bass up to 18½ inches long.

"We've found bass up to 18½ inches, but I'm sure there are bigger ones in the lake," Bush said. "There is a large number of bass that are a nice fighting size."

Tough Day on the Lake

That's what we were after.

Wroblewski, Awe and I launched a 16-foot aluminum fishing boat and began working the shoreline, the weed edges and the tops of the weeds with a variety of tried-and-true bass baits that had paid off on other lakes in the past.

We tried spinner baits, floating minnow baits, pre-rigged plastic worms, scum frogs and live night crawlers. In four hours, all we managed to catch were a couple of sub-legal bass and a few bluegills—all on the live bait.

It was frustrating.

Even so, after thinking things over, Wroblewski and I decided to come back and give it another try, using a different technique, the following evening.

This time, we had better luck.

We used soft stick baits, sold under the names Senko or Sluggo. These are minnow-sized plastic lures that you hook onto a long-shanked hook, burying the tip in the plastic body to fish "weedless."

"This is one of the most weedy lakes you're ever going to fish," Wroblewski said. "You can rig a stick bait, cast it, let it sink, and twitch it back through the weeds to trigger a strike."

That, basically, was all we did that evening in many of the same spots that had failed to produce a day before. There was one other difference worth mentioning—the water had warmed up quickly overnight from 62 to 71 degrees.

This time, in just two hours of fishing before sundown, we caught and released three good-sized bass that ranged from about 14 to 16½ inches long.

Although it's not mandatory, catch and release bass fishing is a good idea on Lower Spring Lake.

"I'd encourage people to catch and release bass as a way of recycling the fish for other anglers to catch," Bush said. "It also provides necessary predation on bluegills to keep that population healthy."

If you want a fish fry, bring home some of those bluegills.

BROWNS LAKE/RACINE COUNTY

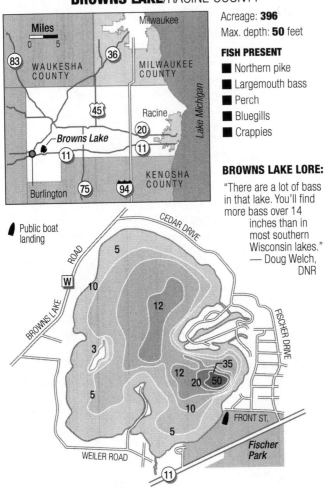

Acreage: **396**
Max. depth: **50** feet

FISH PRESENT

■ Northern pike
■ Largemouth bass
■ Perch
■ Bluegills
■ Crappies

BROWNS LAKE LORE:

"There are a lot of bass in that lake. You'll find more bass over 14 inches than in most southern Wisconsin lakes."
— Doug Welch, DNR

Browns Lake

BURLINGTON—In the soft glow of sunset, something smacked the plastic worm I was reeling over the top of an underwater weed bed on the south end of Browns Lake.

I set the hook, felt a tug and watched in wonder as a healthy largemouth bass came rocketing out of the lake for a top-water tail dance.

It splashed down, but the aerial maneuvers weren't over. This line-stretching largemouth became airborne two more times before I was able to reel it to boat-side.

"I love it when they jump," I told Pat Ehlers, who witnessed the scene from the other end of the boat.

Ehlers, of Franklin, had offered to show me a sample of the summer evening bass action on Browns Lake, one of his favorite local lakes.

"I like the fact that it's close to town," Ehlers told me. "It's got a healthy population of largemouths, and it's a great place to go in the evening for a few hours to catch some fish."

Located in southwestern Racine County, Browns Lake is a 396-acre lake with a maximum depth of 50 feet. There are no boat rentals, but Racine County operates a public boat launch at Fischer Park on the south end of the lake.

In addition to largemouth bass, the lake has naturally reproducing populations of northern pike, bluegills, crappies, perch and pumpkinseeds, according to Doug Welch of the DNR.

The DNR began stocking 19,000 walleyes a year in 2002 to establish a walleye fishery. The walleyes, which are stocked as two-inch fingerlings, should start reaching the legal 15-inch length by about 2006, Welch predicted.

Since the late 1980s, a special bass regulation has been in effect on the lake that sets the minimum length for bass at 16 inches.

"The idea is to protect the bass fishery from over-exploitation and increase predation on a stunted bluegill population," Welch explained.

The regulation has improved the bluegill population, which now includes fish up to eight inches long, and also produced some bigger bass.

Pat Ehlers gets ready to release a largemouth bass from Browns Lake in Racine County.

"There are a lot of bass in that lake," Welch said. "You'll find more bass over 14 inches than in most southern Wisconsin lakes."

Unfortunately, he said: "There are not a lot of bass over 16 inches because they get harvested once they reach that minimum size."

Browns Lake is a heavily used lake with lots of water skiers, jet skiers and pleasure boaters. Because of all the traffic, fishing is best early in the morning or at night.

"You don't see many anglers out there in the middle of the day," Welch said.

We launched Ehlers's boat an hour or so before sundown one July evening and fished into the darkness.

Ehlers, who operates the Fly Fishers shop in West Allis, used a fly-fishing outfit to throw top-water or wet flies, while I used medium-light spinning gear to cast plastic worms.

Both methods worked, but the fishing action picked up considerably after the sun went down and the boat traffic subsided.

We ended up catching and releasing a total of seven bass, up to about 14 inches long, and lost another half dozen or so that somehow managed to get off the hook.

"On a typical evening, fishing sundown till 10 or 11 P.M., catching 20 fish is not out of the ordinary," Ehlers said. "Most of the fish I catch are 11 to 14 inches, but I'll catch maybe a half-dozen bass in the 17- to 18-inch range all season."

That kind of action, coupled with the close proximity to his home, keeps Ehlers coming back to Browns Lake for more.

"You can go out for a few hours, have some fun, catch some nice fish and get back home at a reasonable hour," he said.

LAKE FIVE/WASHINGTON COUNTY

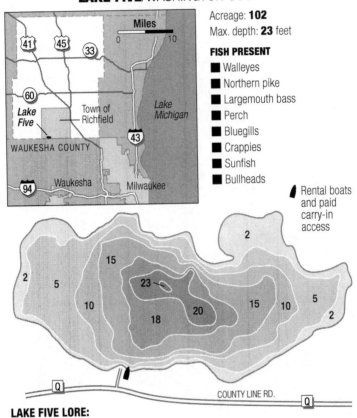

Acreage: **102**
Max. depth: **23** feet

FISH PRESENT

- Walleyes
- Northern pike
- Largemouth bass
- Perch
- Bluegills
- Crappies
- Sunfish
- Bullheads

Rental boats and paid carry-in access

LAKE FIVE LORE:

"The 14-inch size limit on bass has probably helped this lake."
— John Nelson, DNR

Lake Five

L AKE FIVE—If you're looking for a quiet little lake where you can rent a boat, row all the way around in a few hours and catch bluegills, largemouth bass and maybe even a northern pike, you should visit Lake Five.

Located just north of Highway Q, the Waukesha-Washington county line, west of Colgate, Lake Five is a clear, 102-acre lake with a maximum depth of 23 feet.

There is no public launch, but that's not a problem.

For more than 30 years, Shirley Sherwin has operated the Lake Five Boat Livery on the south shore of the lake. For $15, you can rent one of her 20 aluminum rowboats and spend some quality time on the lake.

That's what my wife, Elise, and I did one July evening. It was our first time on Lake Five. But, even though we were newcomers, we caught enough bluegills and bass to make us want to come back for more.

According to John Nelson of the DNR, not much fish management takes place on the lake.

"Because there is no public launch, we do not stock Lake Five," he explained.

Decades ago, largemouth bass were planted in the lake, but there has been no DNR stocking in modern times, Nelson said.

The last DNR fish survey was conducted in 1975, Nelson said. At that time, the survey found largemouth bass up to 20 inches long, but only a few bass over 14 inches and lots of them in the six- to eight-inch range.

The survey also found self-sustaining populations of northern pike, perch, crappies, sunfish, bullheads and bluegills. The bluegills surveyed, while abundant, were only up to about six inches long.

"Basically, the lake has always had a lot of complaints about stunted bluegills," Nelson explained.

In an attempt to curb that problem, the DNR issued permits to a private group to stock walleyes in the lake in the mid-1990s to thin out the bluegills and produce a healthier population. The impact of the walleyes on the bluegills has not been measured.

Aluminum boats can be rented at the Lake Five Boat Livery, located next to the lake on Highway Q, which separates Waukesha and Washington counties.

But, as a side effect, Nelson said, anglers have the potential of possibly landing an occasional walleye.

Even with its abundance of small bass and bluegills, Lake Five is not necessarily a slow-growth lake.

"It may just be that the lake is close to a population center and people take the cream off the top of the fishery," he said. "But even on those lakes, there is the potential to grow bigger fish."

Nelson speculated that a 14-inch minimum size limit, which was established for bass on most southern Wisconsin lakes in 1989, may be producing bigger bass on Lake Five.

"The 14-inch size limit on bass probably has helped this lake," he said.

A temperature study conducted by volunteers in July of 1997 found there wasn't much change in water temperature from the surface to 18 feet down.

"That means you may not get a concentration of fish at a certain depth," Nelson said. "The fish will be scattered."

We found fish just about all over the lake, starting with the shoreline shallows.

We used light-action spinning gear to suspend half a night crawler and a split-shot a couple feet down from a stick bobber. We cast to the lily pads, shady piers and weed pockets along the shore and caught lots of bluegills, plus a few bass.

Our best action came along a shoreline area near a sharp drop-off. So we took off the bobbers and drifted over the nearby deeper water, dragging our bait along the bottom.

That method produced some bigger fish.

We didn't keep any, but I'd say close to half of the 30 or so bluegills we caught would have been big enough to fillet.

And on one of those deep-water drifts, Elise caught and released the fish of the day—a beautiful largemouth bass that must have been more than 17 inches long.

SCHOOL SECTION/PRETTY LAKES/WAUKESHA COUNTY

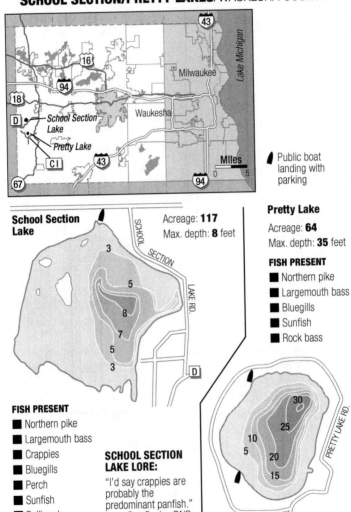

School Section Lake

Acreage: **117**
Max. depth: **8** feet

Pretty Lake

Acreage: **64**
Max. depth: **35** feet

FISH PRESENT
- Northern pike
- Largemouth bass
- Bluegills
- Sunfish
- Rock bass

Public boat
landing with
parking

FISH PRESENT
- Northern pike
- Largemouth bass
- Crappies
- Bluegills
- Perch
- Sunfish
- Bullheads

SCHOOL SECTION LAKE LORE:
"I'd say crappies are probably the predominant panfish."
— Sue Beyler, DNR

Pretty and School Section Lakes

DOUSMAN—If you like small lakes where you can get away from the crowd, fish all the way around in a few hours and maybe catch a few fish, consider adding School Section and Pretty lakes to your list.

Don Streeter and I spent a September day exploring both of these western Waukesha County lakes.

When we launched Streeter's boat at the newly improved boat landing and fishing pier off School Section Road on the north side of School Section Lake, we found ourselves floating in dark water lined by thick expanses of lily pads.

That mass of vegetation might scare off some anglers, but Streeter viewed it as both an opportunity and a challenge.

"This looks like a good lake for slop fishing," he said.

"Slop" is a term used to describe the thickest of thick aquatic plants that most fishing lures would never make it through. But when fished patiently with the right equipment, Streeter demonstrated, slop can produce largemouth bass.

Sue Beyler with the DNR said the lake has lingering water clarity and weed problems resulting from a lake association dredging project in the late 1990s. "They dredged it for about two years straight," she said.

School Section is a 117-acre lake. Although reference books list its maximum depth at just eight feet, the dredging deepened part of the east-central basin to 20 feet.

"I'm not impressed with the dredging," Beyler said. "It created so much turbidity for such a long time."

A DNR survey in 2001 showed "decent numbers of bass and crappies," Beyler said, although both the size and quantity of the fish were less than optimal.

"I'd say crappies were probably the predominant panfish," she said.

Don Streeter releases a largemouth bass he caught in heavy weeds using a snag-proof plastic frog back into School Section Lake.

The DNR stocks 585 northern pike fingerlings every year to support a natural population. In addition to bass and crappies, the lake also has self-sustaining populations of bluegills, perch, sunfish and bullheads.

Beyler believes the lake's water clarity and weed problems should be addressed.

"As long as they created that deep area, we'd like to see it productive for fishing," she said. "It's not going to be if it has turbid water and it's choked with weeds."

All in the Frogs

Even with those conditions, Streeter and I managed to find a few bass, including an impressive 17-incher.

For slop fishing, Streeter uses snag-proof plastic frogs with weedless hooks sold under various brand names, including "Scum Frog" and "Mighty Mike."

We each tied a frog to a strong, low-stretch line called Fire Line. "It has the strength of 16-pound-test with the diameter of six-pound mono," Streeter said. "When bass are buried in the weeds, you need strong line to pull them out."

We made long casts into the weeds, then slowly worked the frogs back over the tops of the pads, pausing at edges and openings.

"You can hop it and stop it and let it sit there to entice the fish," Streeter said. "It's an exciting way to fish. It keeps your mind involved. You never know when that fish is going to hit."

When a bass strikes, the splashing and commotion can trick you into attempting a hook-set too early. "The absolute most important thing is to wait until you feel the fish before you set the hook," Streeter said. "If you pull the lure away too soon, the fish won't be able to locate it again in the weeds."

We spent about three hours on School Section Lake, catching and releasing three bass—a 10-, 15- and that 17-incher—plus a 20-inch northern.

Earlier that day, we paid a visit to nearby Pretty Lake, a 64-acre lake with a maximum depth of 35 feet.

Pretty Lake has two small, hard-to-find boat landings, both off Pretty Lake Road. "Between the two launches you could get five boats on the lake and that's our minimum for adequate access," Beyler said.

The launch we used was poorly marked, had limited parking, a dirt ramp and shallow water that made it difficult, but not impossible, to launch Streeter's fishing boat.

No Stocking

Pretty Lake has natural populations of largemouth bass, northern pike, bluegills, sunfish and rock bass. The DNR does no stocking. A fish survey in spring of 1998 showed bass up to 15 inches, northerns up to 19 inches, and panfish "up to five or six inches, tops," Beyler said.

"For a while, in the '80s and '90s, that lake had a temporary 16-inch minimum for bass," Beyler said. "It was a study to see if the bass would control the bluegill population."

The conclusion was that the special regulation had little impact on the panfish population, so it was removed in 1999.

Streeter and I spent a couple hours throwing plastic worms at the shoreline structure and over weed beds with marginal results. We caught and released four fish—two sub-legal largemouths, a rock bass and a small northern.

"A lot of the shoreline water was very shallow, so it didn't hold many fish," Streeter said.

We might have done better, Beyler suggested, by fishing mid-lake.

"That lake is kind of like a bowl," she said. "There is an outside weed line in about ten feet of water. You would probably have a better chance of finding more bass out there."

There's something to keep in mind for next time.

ASHIPPUN LAKE/WAUKESHA COUNTY

Acreage: **84**
Max. depth: **40** feet

FISH PRESENT
- Northern pike
- Largemouth bass
- Perch
- Bluegills
- Crappies

ASHIPPUN LAKE LORE:
"Most people fish northern pike and panfish in winter and largemouth bass in summer."
— Sue Beyler, DNR

Ashippun River Park

LAKE SIDE HEIGHTS CT.

Mc MAHON RD.

Public boat landing

LAKE SIDE HEIGHTS DR.

Ashippun Lake

OCONOMOWOC—In the fading sun of evening, I was casting a spinner blade along the outside edge of a clump of lily pads in the nearshore water of Ashippun Lake when another fish hit.

I set the hook and a largemouth bass became airborne, tail dancing and head shaking before splashing down.

"I've got a jumper," I told Don Streeter, who was busy casting at the other end of the boat.

As if on cue, the black bass erupted from the water one more time and dived for the weeds before I was able to bring it to the boat, carefully remove the hook and watch it swim away.

"How many is that," I asked. "Fifteen or sixteen?"

Neither of us could say for sure, which meant that we were having a pretty good afternoon of fishing on pretty little Ashippun Lake.

Ashippun is an 84-acre, spring-fed lake with a maximum depth of 40 feet, located in the northwest corner of Waukesha County, north of Oconomowoc. There are no boat rentals, but Waukesha County Parks and the DNR operate a free boat launch and picnic area off McMahon Road on the southwest side of the lake.

Hideaway Spot

"It's just far enough out of the way that it doesn't get much attention," said Sue Beyler of the DNR. "It's not right off the freeway. You have to look for it."

Years ago, the DNR used to stock walleyes, but stopped after 1989.

"It's not really a walleye lake," Beyler explained. "It's more of a northern pike, largemouth bass and panfish lake. With hatchery walleyes not being as plentiful, we decided to focus walleye stocking on lakes where there is a reasonable chance of self-sustaining walleye populations."

Since 1991, however, the DNR has stocked about 420 northern pike fingerlings each year to supplement the lake's naturally reproducing northern population.

Don Streeter with a largemouth bass.

"There are quite a few northerns," Beyler said. "The lake has lots of wetland shoreline with cattails and bull rushes, which are both good habitat for northern pike spawning."

Ashippun also has self-sustaining populations of largemouth bass, bluegills, perch, crappies and sunfish. The abundant northern pike and panfish populations make the lake a popular ice fishing spot.

"Most people fish northern pike and panfish in winter and largemouth bass in summer," Beyler said. "Summer pressure seems to be lighter. There are people out there, but you don't see droves of anglers and boaters."

One cool, windy, weekday afternoon in September, Streeter and I practically had the lake to ourselves. We spent about five hours on the water, taking our time to work the shoreline structure all around the lake, plus the deep-water break line on the east end.

Great Day for Fishing

We used medium-action spinning gear with six- or eight-pound monofilament to throw plastic worms or suspend live night crawlers beneath slip bobbers, plus bait-casting rigs with ten-pound monofilament to throw spinner blades.

Just about everything worked.

We focused on largemouth bass and caught them in natural structure—the lily pads, weed pockets and bull rushes on the west end; as well as man-made structure—the piers, docks and moored boats on the east end.

"We caught fish in from 1 to 12 feet of water," Streeter said. "Considering that it was the second day after a cold front moved in, we had tremendous fishing."

We ended up catching and releasing lots of bass up to about 16 inches long, plus two northerns that probably would have measured about 20 and 27 inches.

"It's a very pleasant lake to fish," Streeter said. "It's small enough to work your way around in a half-day without all the traffic and hustle-bustle you find on so many southern Wisconsin lakes. It's a nice little lake to spend some time and have some action."

PINE LAKE/WAUKESHA COUNTY

PINE LAKE LORE:
"Usually we don't see lakes with good populations of largemouth and smallmouth bass, but this lake has them both."
— Sue Beyler, DNR

Acreage: **703**
Max. depth: **85** feet

FISH PRESENT
- ■ Northern pike
- ■ Walleyes
- ■ Largemouth bass
- ■ Smallmouth bass
- ■ Perch
- ■ Bluegills
- ■ Crappies
- ■ Cisco

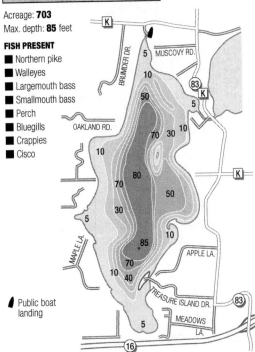

🔻 Public boat landing

Pine Lake

C HENEQUA—We'd been fishing the choppy waters of Pine Lake for about a hour, catching a few bluegills and small bass, when there was a substantial tug on the night crawler at the end of my line.

The brick-wall resistance I encountered when setting the hook was a sign that things were picking up.

The fish made some strong, underwater runs before shifting gears and skyrocketing out of the water so close to the boat that we almost felt the splash.

A quick, profile glimpse of a green-bronze flank, a red gill and a fiery-orange eye gave visual confirmation of what I already knew in my heart: This was a good smallmouth bass, a fish that, pound for pound, fights longer and harder than just about anything that swims.

There were more hard runs and, of course, a last-minute power-dive under the boat before I was able to steer the battling bass into the net waiting in Bob Bayha's hands.

"Somebody always gets a nice one," Bayha said as I released the fish.

Bayha, of Brown Deer, and his friend, Ray Guarascio, of Menomonee Falls, have fished Pine Lake together for years.

"One day about five or six years ago, we came out here and really smoked the bass," Bayha said. "We've been coming back ever since."

Great Lake

Pine Lake is a clear, 703-acre lake with a maximum depth of 85 feet and a reputation for producing a variety of fish.

"People go there and, most of the time, they catch fish," said Sue Beyler of the DNR.

Part of the reason may be the lake's diverse habitat.

"There are some nice, shallow bays for panfish and largemouth bass, some good weed beds and a lot of steep drop-offs," Beyler said. "There are places where you're not much more than 30 feet from shore and the water is already 30 feet deep."

Bob Bayha (left) and Ray Guarascio are a short distance from the shore, but the depth could be as much as 30 feet at Pine Lake.

The sharp drop-offs along the eastern shoreline would be a good place to jig for walleyes, Beyler suggested.

There are no boat rentals, but there is one public boat launch, operated by the Village of Chenequa, off Highway K on the north end of the lake.

Before 1995, the DNR did not stock Pine Lake because the old launch was in disrepair and parking was inadequate.

"The DNR can't do fisheries management in a lake that doesn't have adequate public access," Beyler said. "That means a way to get a boat in, and parking within a quarter mile. That wasn't the case on Pine Lake prior to the mid-1990s."

Well-stocked Lake

Since the new launch was built, however, the DNR has stocked between 2,000 and 3,500 northern pike fingerlings each year, and between 35,000 and 70,000 walleye fingerlings every other year.

"There is natural reproduction of both walleyes and northerns," Beyler said. "We stock to keep the population levels up with the increased fishing pressure resulting from the new launch."

In addition, the lake has self-sustaining populations of largemouth and smallmouth bass, bluegills, crappies, sunfish, perch and bullheads.

"Most people fish crappies on the north end of the lake in the evening in fall," Beyler said.

Bass fishing can be good all summer long.

"Usually we don't see lakes with good populations of largemouth and smallmouth bass, but this lake has them both," Beyler said.

For our trip, Bayha, Guarascio and I went after the smallmouths. We used medium-action spinning gear with six- to eight-pound mono line, dressed a number six or eight hook with a night crawler and pinched a split-shot a foot or so up from the crawler. Bayha threaded a little red "attractor" bead above his hook, Guarascio tied on a chartreuse spinner rig, and I went with a crawler on a plain hook.

We did our best to anchor the boat along a steep, near-shore break line so we could fish the bottom in about 20 to 25 feet of water. It was windy, so that was harder than it sounds.

We had to reposition the boat several times, but when we presented our bait at the right depth, we caught fish.

We spent a pleasant morning on the lake, catching and releasing about 15 smallmouth bass, up to about 16 inches long, plus a few bonus bluegills.

"I've always had pretty good luck out here," Bayha said. "That's why I keep coming back."

GREEN LAKE/GREEN LAKE COUNTY

Acreage: **7,346**
Max. depth: **236** feet

FISH PRESENT

- Northern pike
- Walleyes
- Crappies
- Smallmouth bass
- Largemouth bass
- Lake trout
- Brown trout

- Muskies
- Bluegills
- Sunfish
- Perch
- White bass
- Cisco

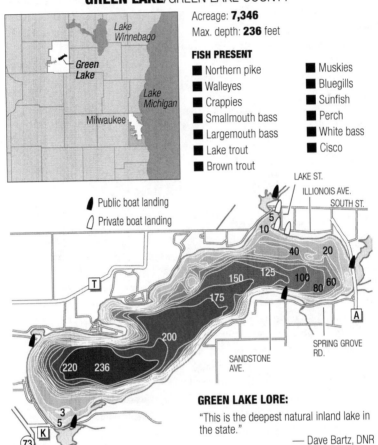

- Public boat landing
- Private boat landing

LAKE ST.
ILLIONOIS AVE.
SOUTH ST.

5
10
40   20
150   125
100   60
175   80

T

200

A

220   236

SANDSTONE
AVE.

SPRING GROVE
RD.

3
5

K

73

GREEN LAKE LORE:

"This is the deepest natural inland lake in
the state."

— Dave Bartz, DNR

Big Green Lake

GREEN LAKE—Like a big, deep-green mystery, Green Lake holds the promise of endless variety and year-round fishing opportunity.

"No matter what time of year, there's going to be some type of game fish that's active," Randy Butters told me when I met up with him at the Deacon Mills Park boat landing on the northeast side of the lake one August morning.

Butters, of Ripon, has been fishing Green Lake all his life. These days, he concentrates on smallmouth bass and panfish. But, through the years, he has trolled for lake trout in summer, fished the weed lines for walleyes and northern pike in the fall, and caught lake trout, walleyes and ciscoes through the ice in winter.

Green Lake is a 7,346-acre lake with a maximum depth of 236 feet.

"It's the deepest natural inland lake in the state," said Dave Bartz, Department of Natural Resources fisheries biologist at Montello.

According to Bartz, Green Lake has naturally reproducing populations of walleyes, northern pike, smallmouth and largemouth bass, bluegills, sunfish, perch, crappies, white bass and ciscoes.

To bolster the lake's low-density walleye population, the Green Lake Chapter of Walleyes for Tomorrow has been stocking millions of tiny walleye fry since the late 1990s.

"We get reports from fishermen that they're catching small walleyes, but they haven't turned up in our surveys, so we haven't documented any success from that program," Bartz said.

The lake also has a small musky population, due to stocking by local musky clubs.

"Guys fishing for big northerns with chubs or suckers occasionally catch a musky," Bartz said. "The lake has the potential to produce big ones. In 1998, we caught a 52-inch musky during a spring fyke net survey."

Trout Hotbed

In addition, Bartz said, the DNR has been maintaining a lake trout fishery since the 1940s.

Randy Butters, who's been fishing Green Lake all of his life, removes a jig from the jaws of a smallmouth bass.

"In recent years, we've stocked an average of between 15,000 to 25,000 lake trout annually," he said. "This year, for the first time, we're going to be stocking the Trout Lake strain of lake trout from Vilas County."

Trout from state hatcheries are brought to a co-op facility maintained by Green Lake County with support from the DNR. Fingerlings are kept at the facility from August till March, when they are released into the lake as five-to nine-inch fish.

"A lot of guides target the lake trout," Bartz said. "We've been looking for a second species of cold water trout."

So, to supplement the lake trout fishery, the DNR began stocking the Seeforellen brown trout strain in the late 1990s, and, so far, they seem to be doing well.

"We're starting to get reports of them being caught up to about 20 inches," Bartz said. "Some of those fish have been doubling in size, year to year."

In addition to Deacon Mills Park, other major boat landing locations include Highway A near the inlet on the east side of the lake, Horner Road on the southeast side, Dodge Memorial Park off Highway K on the southwest end, and Beyer's Cove Road off Highway 73 in the northwest corner. Most launches cost $4.

Boat rentals are available at three business in Green Lake. Green Lake Marina, 485 Park Drive, and Bay View Motel, 439 Lake Street, each charge $65 a day for a fishing boat and motor. The Heidel House, 643 Illinois Avenue, charges $250 a day.

Going for Smallmouth

Green Lake doesn't have a lot of shallow, lily-pad bays that are typically associated with largemouth bass. As a result, Bartz said: "The smallmouth bass are a little more predominant."

Butters and I looked for smallmouths along the sharp shoreline drop-offs.

"There are a lot of sheer cliffs underneath the water surface," Butters explained. "You can be 30 to 40 feet from shore and in 30 feet of water."

And that deep water can hold fish.

"It's not like most lakes where you fish a maximum depth of 10 or 12 feet down," Butters said. "It's not uncommon to fish 35 feet down for small-mouths.

We found our first few bass in one of those near-shore deep water spots. We tied ⅛-ounce jigs to medium-action spinning gear with eight-pound monofilament line and dressed the jig with either a leech or a piece of night crawler.

We used an electric trolling motor and a depth finder to try and hold the boat in a narrow band of water only a few feet wide where the fish were biting.

"It seemed like all the fish were at about 20 feet of water," Butters said. "You really have to pinpoint your spots."

When we presented bait at the right depth, we got bites.

We tried a few other spots and found more bass along the weed lines in 12 to 14 feet of water.

By quitting time, we had caught and released about ten smallmouth bass, plus one largemouth bass and a few perch and bluegills.

"Green Lake is a challenging lake to fish," Butters said. "You have to put in some time to learn it. But it pays off."

LAKE COLUMBIA/COLUMBIA COUNTY

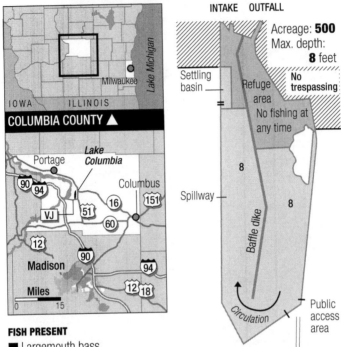

INTAKE   OUTFALL

Acreage: **500**
Max. depth:
8 feet

No trespassing

Settling basin

Refuge area
No fishing at any time

Spillway

Baffle dike

8

8

Circulation

Public access area

VJ

COLUMBIA COUNTY ▲

Lake Columbia

Portage

Columbus

90   94   16   151

VJ   51

60

12

90

Madison

94

Miles
0   15

12   18

IOWA   ILLINOIS

Milwaukee

Lake Michigan

FISH PRESENT
- ■ Largemouth bass
- ■ Smallmouth bass
- ■ Hybrid striped bass
- ■ Bluegills
- ■ Bullheads
- ■ Channel catfish
- ■ Flathead catfish

LAKE COLUMBIA LORE:

"It's the only lake in Wisconsin with hybrid striped bass."

– Tim Larson, DNR

Lake Columbia

PORTAGE—Lake Columbia offers some unique year-round fishing opportunities.

Because this lake is actually a 500-acre cooling reservoir for the Columbia Electric Generating Station, a coal-fired power plant operated by Alliant Energy Corp., the water remains open all year, even in the coldest winter months.

There is a carry-in-only boat access, suitable for small boats, canoes and float tubes, off Highway J on the south end of the lake. Except for the power plant and two well-marked fish refuges at the north end, the rest of the mile-and-a-quarter-long lake is open to shore fishing.

The lake has self-sustaining populations of largemouth and smallmouth bass, bluegills, bullheads, and both channel and flathead catfish.

And, according to Tim Larson, fisheries biologist with the Department of Natural Resources at Poynette: "It's the only lake in Wisconsin with hybrid striped bass."

The hybrid striper, Larson said, is a fast-growing cross between an ocean striped bass and a white bass that is popular among anglers in southern states.

"The cross can tolerate warm water," Larson explained.

That's why the DNR stocks the lake with about six thousand four-inch fingerlings each fall.

"We buy them from a private hatchery in Missouri," Larson said. "The power company donates money so we can buy the hybrids every year."

Although a DNR survey in fall of 2002 turned up plenty of hybrid stripers in the 12- to 14-inch range, they can reach 13 pounds and bigger. The state record is a 13-pound, 14.2-ounce striper caught in March of 2002.

The DNR manages the lake for trophy largemouth and smallmouth bass, and hybrid striper bass. Special regulations call for catch and release for all three species for anything less than 18 inches. The daily bag limit is one largemouth, or one smallmouth, bass—plus three hybrid bass—all longer than 18 inches.

The survey also found lots of largemouth bass in the 12- to 17-inch range, but few legal largemouth bass and not very many smallmouth bass.

Hybrid stripers are a cross between an ocean striped bass and a white bass.

"It's probably 90 percent largemouths," Larson said of the bass fishery.

Aside from a narrow dike that runs right up the middle, the lake is virtually devoid of structure, and the depth is "a pretty uniform seven feet," Larson said.

"It's so hot that there is no aquatic vegetation," Larson said. "The panfish never grow to keeper size."

In winter, the lake is often shrouded in an eerie fog caused when the hot water meets the cold air. The lake is most heavily fished in January, February and early March, Larson said: "because there is nowhere else to fish, other than ice fishing."

All summer long, however, anglers continue to fish for catfish.

"There are tons of small catfish and bullheads," Larson said. There also are some big catfish, including flatheads 20 to 40 inches long.

Trolling with either electric or outboard motors is allowed. Boat anglers tend to fish along the dike, while shore anglers cast from the shoreline rocks.

Water temperature can be the key to finding fish.

"There's about a 25-degree temperature differential between the intake and the discharge at the plant," Larson said. "If you want to bass fish, bring a thermometer with you. If you find 70- to 75-degree water, that's where you'll find the bass."

Don Streeter and I decided to shore fish Lake Columbia one March day.

We parked at the carry-in launch and walked south, using medium-action spinning gear to cast a variety of plugs, spinners and live bait from the shoreline rocks.

We jumped from spot to spot, but couldn't buy a bite. It wasn't until we switched directions and made a long hike to the other end of the lake—all the way to the warm water area on the north end—that we started to catch fish.

Half a night crawler on a small hook weighted with a couple pieces of split-shot, so you could slowly drag it across the bottom, was all it took.

In about an hour's time, that method produced enough channel catfish for a fish fry, plus three under-sized hybrid striped bass, which we released. The stripers looked like white bass, only a little more long and narrow.

"When we found the warmest water, we found the active fish," Streeter said.

That was the key.

Walleyes

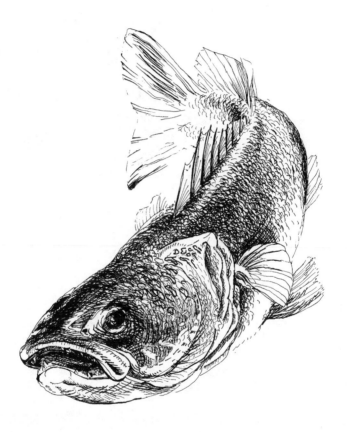

J. Riepenhoff

Walleyes

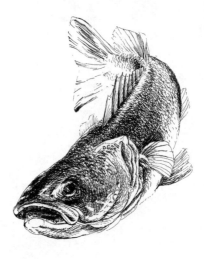

J. Riepenhoff

WALLEYES may not be the most spectacular fighting fish. They rarely jump, opting instead to dive or just put on the brakes and resist.

Still, when you get a big one on the line, figure on spending some time bringing it to the net. I caught my biggest walleye, an 11-pounder, while trolling a crank bait in Sturgeon Bay at night.

Wisconsin anglers love walleyes. Anyone who has ever waited in line at a boat launch during one of the spring walleye spawning runs on the Fox, Wolf, Rock or Wisconsin rivers can attest to the popularity of this fish.

Maybe that's because walleyes make such excellent table fare. Grilled, baked or deep-fried, a walleye fillet is hard to beat.

Although walleyes are more common in the north, there are many good walleye fishing opportunities in southern Wisconsin.

Walleyes can be finicky biters that are hard to hook. Unlike other game fish, walleyes bite only when they are hungry and cannot be coaxed into an aggravation bite.

That may be why many anglers use live bait, including a night crawler, leech or minnow. Popular live bait methods include vertical jigging off the lake bottom, presenting live bait suspended beneath a slip-bobber rig or trolling a night crawler behind a spinner or in a "crawler harness." When jigging, especially in spring, I use a stinger hook—a small treble hook tied to the jig with a short piece of monofilament line—to hook light biters.

Using planer boards to troll crank baits that imitate the forage fish can also be deadly. If you're serious about trolling for walleyes, it's worth investing in some line-counter reels and a crank bait reference book that combine to let you run your lures at precise depths.

The Lake Winnebago system is an excellent place to catch walleyes, and open water fishing starts there as soon as the ice is out.

In spring and fall, look for walleyes in less than ten feet of water, near green weeds, rock bars, mud flats and underwater bars or humps.

As summer heats up, you'll find them in the same kinds of structure, only in deeper water, down to 30 feet or more, depending on the lake. Also in summer, walleyes sometimes suspend in deep water near the thermocline, the place where the warm surface water meets the cool, deep water. Look for clouds of bait fish on your locater and the walleyes won't be far off.

In winter, many walleyes are taken on jigging spoons, artificial jigging minnows or tip-ups baited with a live fathead or shiner minnow.

Winnebago, Poygan, Winneconne, Koshkonong, La Belle and Pike lakes are profiled in this chapter.

LAKE WINNEBAGO/FOND DU LAC COUNTY

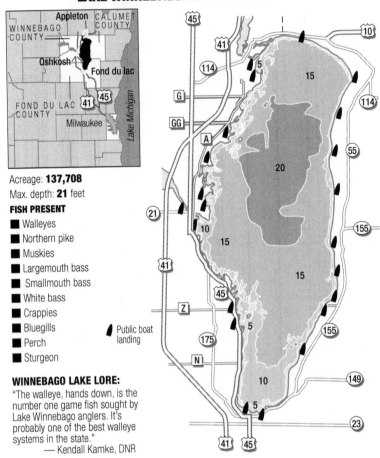

Acreage: **137,708**
Max. depth: **21** feet

FISH PRESENT

- ■ Walleyes
- ■ Northern pike
- ■ Muskies
- ■ Largemouth bass
- ■ Smallmouth bass
- ■ White bass
- ■ Crappies
- ■ Bluegills
- ■ Perch
- ■ Sturgeon

◢ Public boat landing

WINNEBAGO LAKE LORE:

"The walleye, hands down, is the number one game fish sought by Lake Winnebago anglers. It's probably one of the best walleye systems in the state."
— Kendall Kamke, DNR

Lake Winnebago

BLACK WOLF—As we trolled along the western shoreline of Lake Winnebago, the "tattle flag" on one of the planer boards went down, and Randy Butters grabbed the rod from its holder and started to reel.

When a fish surfaced way out behind the boat, I could see that it was a lot longer than the white bass we'd been catching all afternoon, so I reached for the net.

It took a while for Butters to work the fish—a big northern—to the back of the boat. When he finally did, the fish barely fit into the small hoop of the long-handled walleye net.

Somehow I made the scoop.

After a couple quick pictures, we released the northern, which measured about 33 inches and must have weighed about 11 pounds.

"I thought we were snagged at first," guide Gordy Chmielewski said as we watched the big northern swim off. "That was a good sized fish."

According to Kendall Kamke, senior fisheries biologist with the Department of Natural Resources at Oshkosh, northerns show up as occasional bonus fish for Lake Winnebago anglers.

"The walleye, hands down, is the number one game fish sought by Lake Winnebago anglers," Kamke said. "It's probably one of the best walleye systems in the state."

The daily bag limit is five and there is no size limit for walleyes.

"We don't need a size limit," Kamke said. "Reproduction is good, the growth rate is good and there are adequate numbers of small fish. Winnebago has historically been a lake where people go to get walleyes to eat, and the 14- to 16-inchers are perfect eating fish."

Walleye reproduction has been good each spring since 1990, Kamke said, especially in 1996, which he called "the largest year class of walleyes since standardized sampling began in 1986."

Randy Butters (left) unhooks a white bass, and Gordy Chmielewski sets up a planer board on Lake Winnebago.

Many Approaches

For walleyes, hook-and-line fishing remains open year-round, so walleye fishing begins in spring, as soon as the ice is out and the walleyes return from their river spawning runs.

"In early May, a guy can put on waders, wade the shoreline, twitch a Rapala and catch a lot of walleyes," Kamke said.

Others prefer to fish near shore with live bait and a slip bobber.

Trolling starts along the rock reefs in late spring and continues all summer long, although schools of feeding walleyes can be hard to find once they move to mud flats as summer wears on.

"Up until mid-July this year, the walleye bite was phenomenal," said Chmielewski, who has guided on the lake since 1995. "You could go out there and catch a limit of 18 to 20 inchers in a couple hours."

At 137,708 acres, Lake Winnebago is Wisconsin's largest inland lake. It has a maximum depth of 21 feet and an average depth of about 15 feet.

The lake has self-sustaining populations of walleyes, northerns, large-mouth and smallmouth bass, perch, bluegills, black and white crappies, sunfish, white bass, sheepshead, yellow bass, plus a few muskies.

Sauger fishing has been closed on the lake since the late 1990s in an attempt to help the lake's struggling sauger population recover.

Perch fishing is also popular. Anglers try to locate a school, often in 6 to 12 feet of water near rocks or where the gravel meets the mud.

"Just go where all the other boats are," Kamke advised, and work a jig on the bottom with a red worm or hellgrammite.

Largemouth bass fishermen fish the channels or shallow, weedy bays with a plastic worm or spinner bait, while smallmouth anglers present live bait or a crank bait along the rock reefs in deeper water.

"Lake Winnebago also has one of few self-sustaining sturgeon populations in North America where an annual harvest is allowed," Kamke said. "Spearing is the only legal way to take a sturgeon."

A sturgeon spearing season is held through the ice in February. Spearers need a special license and tag. In recent years, due to harvest quotas established to protect the sturgeon population, the season has been as short as two days.

There are more than 30 boat landings around the lake. Launch sites include Menominee Park, 24th Avenue, and Fugleberg Street in Oshkosh; Asylum Point, north of Oshkosh; Rec Park in Neenah; Jefferson Park in Menasha; High Cliff State Park, west of Sherwood on the northeast side; Calumet County Park; Stockbridge Harbor; Quinney; Brothertown Harbor;

Columbia Park in Pipe; Fisherman's Road off Highway 151, north of Peebles; Lakeside West Park in Fond du Lac; and Nagy Park/Black Wolf, south of Oshkosh off Highway 45.

Boat rentals are available at the Willows Resort in Van Dyne, six miles north of Fond du Lac on Highway 45, on the west side of the lake.

Trolling for Walleyes

Chmielewski, Butters and I launched at the boat landing in the Town of Black Wolf on a hot and humid August afternoon. We trolled crank baits along the outside edges of rock reefs in 6 to 12 feet of water on the west side of the lake.

Trolling requires special equipment. We used line-counter reels, which let you calculate the depth that a lure will run, strung with 14-pound-test monofilament. We also used Off Shore "tattle flags" with a spring-loaded mechanism that makes the flag go down to signal when you have a fish on the line.

In about five hours, we only managed to catch one 14-inch walleye. But we had almost constant action with white bass, catching and releasing close to 30. And that big northern was a nice surprise.

We saw lots of other boats on the water, but never felt crowded.

"It gets a lot of angler pressure, but it's not over-fished," Kamke said. "Because of it's size and productivity, it can handle the fishing pressure."

LAC La BELLE LAKE/WAUKESHA COUNTY

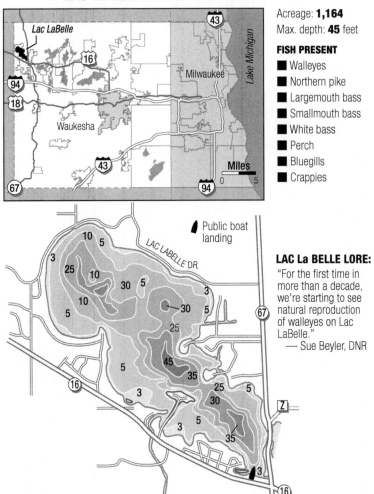

Acreage: **1,164**
Max. depth: **45** feet

FISH PRESENT
- Walleyes
- Northern pike
- Largemouth bass
- Smallmouth bass
- White bass
- Perch
- Bluegills
- Crappies

LAC La BELLE LORE:
"For the first time in more than a decade, we're starting to see natural reproduction of walleyes on Lac LaBelle."
— Sue Beyler, DNR

Lac La Belle

O CONOMOWOC—Slowly, patiently and with utmost concentration, Gary Wroblewski tapped a jig and leech on the bottom of Lac La Belle, alongside the edge of an underwater weed bed.

"There's a fish," he suddenly announced, setting the hook and putting a major bend in his fishing rod. "Get the net."

Before too long, I was able to scoop up his walleye, a fish that was about 17 inches long.

On most lakes when you catch a walleye like that, it soon becomes a fillet. But, after I took a quick picture, Wroblewski released the fish.

"This lake is becoming a quality fishery because of the size restriction on walleyes," he said. "There aren't many lakes in southeastern Wisconsin where you can catch walleyes this size."

He was talking about Lac La Belle's special walleye regulation that sets the daily bag limit at one fish, with a minimum length of 20 inches.

Sue Beyler of the DNR said the special regulation was established in 1991, after a carp removal project on the lake.

"We wanted to boost the game fish population," she said. "Female walleyes weren't spawning until they were 15 or 16 inches long. We felt that we could get some natural reproduction if we protected the adult walleyes."

The plan is paying off.

According to DNR creel surveys, Beyler said: "In 1982, carp were among the top species people fished for. In 1992, the vast majority of people were out there fishing for walleyes."

In addition, she said: "For the first time in more than a decade, we're starting to see natural reproduction of walleyes on Lac La Belle."

The walleye population has grown from one adult fish per two acres in the 1980s, to the current level of two adults per acre.

Lac La Belle is a 1,164-acre lake with a maximum depth of 45 feet. There are no boat rentals, but the City of Oconomowoc operates a public boat launch off Highway 16 on the south end of the lake. There is also a public fishing pier in a city park, east of the launch.

Gary Wroblewski holds a 17-inch walleye from Lac La Belle. He won't take it home because a lake rule sets a minimum length of 20 inches.

Walleyes, Northern Stocked

The DNR stocks one hundred thousand walleye fingerlings every other year, plus five thousand northern pike fingerlings every year. The lake also has largemouth and smallmouth bass, bluegills, crappies, sunfish, perch, rock bass, white bass, channel catfish and muskies.

"We don't stock muskies on Lac La Belle," Beyler said. "We stock them in Okauchee Lake and they come through the Oconomowoc River, Oconomowoc Lake and Fowler Lake to get into Lac La Belle."

La Belle also has a reduced daily bag limit of 15 panfish. "The panfish population is poor," Beyler said. "It's definitely a habitat-related problem. There is not a lot of productive habitat."

The lake has a few weed beds, where fish tend to concentrate, separated by vast expanses without any vegetation.

"There's a big weed area in the northwest bay, a smaller weed bed south of Kohl's Bay on the east side and another one in Kohl's Bay itself," Beyler said. "There are lily pads in the bay on the southwest side that hold bass and panfish, and that's about it."

Because the water can be cloudy, limiting visibility, Wroblewski said: "This is the kind of lake that you need to use your depth finder to constantly monitor the drop-offs or the weed edges."

In addition to the weeds, Beyler said: "Some people fish the drop-offs or the places where long, underwater bars extend from points. People have luck with walleyes and smallmouths along those bars."

Wroblewski sometimes likes to use night crawler harnesses to troll for suspended walleyes along the drop-offs.

Carp Pose Problem

Carp infestation, via the Rock River system, continues to be a problem. Carp, a non-native species, eat fish eggs, churn up sediment and dislodge weeds that game fish need for cover,

In 1986 and 1987, the DNR poisoned and removed almost 120,000 pounds of carp, Beyler said. Afterward, workers released about 10,000 pounds of flathead catfish, ranging from three to ten pounds each, into the lake.

"The idea was for them to prey on carp," said Beyler, noting that the flatheads are protected on the lake, and must be released if caught.

Even so, carp numbers have started to rise again in recent years.

"Carp are probably the number one problem for game fish on that lake," Beyler said.

So the DNR took more action. In winter 2001-2002, an electronic carp barrier, which was installed in the late 1980s but quit working a decade later, was reactivated at the confluence of the Oconomowoc and Rock Rivers.

Beyond that, Beyler said: "We are considering doing some additional carp removals in 2004."

Wroblewski, Larry Awe, and I fished Lac La Belle one recent morning. We concentrated on the big weed bed on the northwest side of the lake in 12 to 15 feet of water.

We put out a few floating markers along the weed edge and used medium-light spinning gear to present live bait—night crawlers, leeches or minnows—along the outside of the weeds, either vertical jigging or suspending the bait beneath a slip bobber.

We missed some strikes and got picked a few times, but ended up catching and releasing two nice walleyes that were 16 and 17 inches long, plus a white bass that was about 14 inches.

"When the bite is on, it's not unusual to catch 10 or 15 walleyes," Wroblewski said. "For the angler looking to hone his skills and catch some nice walleyes, this lake offers a unique opportunity."

POYGAN/WINNECONNE LAKES/WINNEBAGO COUNTY

Detailed Area

FISH PRESENT

- Walleyes
- Northern pike
- Largemouth bass
- Smallmouth bass
- Muskies
- Catfish
- White bass
- Panfish

POYGAN/WINNECONNE LAKE LORE:

"It's a good place to start fishing early in the year. It's shallow. It warms up fast, especially on the north side of the lake. The walleyes come down from the Wolf River after they're done spawning."
– Bill Coats, angler

LAKE POYGAN
Acreage: **14,102**
Max. depth: **11** feet

LAKE WINNECONNE
Acreage: **4,507**
Max. depth: **8** feet

Major public boat landings

Boat rentals

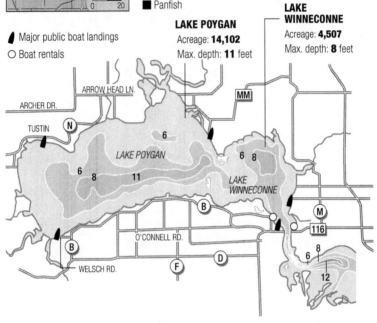

Lakes Poygan and Winneconne

WINNECONNE—We were trolling along the north shore of Lake Winneconne, staring at the planer boards lined up in V-formation in the wake of the boat.

All of a sudden one of the boards popped down and shot backward, as an underwater force pulled it out of line.

"That's a good fish," Bill Coats offered, as he lifted the rod from its holder and handed it to Randy Butters. "Take it easy."

Butters reeled slowly as Coats and I scrambled to clear the other lines and grab the net.

The fish stayed down.

Butters reeled, stopped so Coats could remove the planer board, then reeled some more.

Finally, he brought the fish up to where Coats could scoop it with the net. It was a big, bronze, beautiful 20-inch walleye, our first of the day.

Coats and Butters, both of Ripon, had invited me up to Winnebago County to fish Lake Winneconne one cool, sunny day in May.

"It's a good place to start fishing early in the year," said Coats, who has fished the lake for ten years. "It's shallow. It warms up fast, especially on the north side of the lake. The walleyes come down from the Wolf River after they're done spawning."

Lake Winneconne is a 4,507-acre lake with a maximum depth of just nine feet.

Kendall Kamke with the DNR called Winneconne and the adjacent Lake Poygan "essentially one lake." Back in the early 1900s, a bog separated Winneconne from Poygan, a 14,102-acre lake with a maximum depth of 11 feet. But the bog is long gone.

Randy Butters (left) and Bill Coats remove a crank bait from the jaws of a walleye during their fishing trip on Lake Winneconne.

Variety of Species

Both lakes have diverse, healthy and self-sustaining fish populations, with no stocking required.

"Poygan and Winneconne probably have some of the most diverse fishing of the Lake Winnebago system," Kamke said. "Walleyes and largemouth bass are probably the two main targets for most game fish anglers."

In addition, Kamke said, the fishery includes northern pike, smallmouth bass, catfish, a variety of panfish, plus white bass, sheepshead and even some muskies.

"There is a small, self-sustaining population of muskies," he said. "It's slowly increasing."

The DNR is also reintroducing a once-native strain of Great Lakes spotted musky into the system, Kamke said.

Good Launching Points

The Village of Winneconne operates a boat launch just north of Highway 116 on the west side of the Winneconne bridge and Winnebago County operates another one in Marble Park off N. 3rd, on the east side of the bridge, both in the southeast corner of Lake Winneconne.

Major launches on Lake Poygan include those located on Richter Lane, off Highway MM on the northeast corner of the lake; in Tustin on the northwest end; and at Captain's Cove tavern off Welsch Road in the southwest.

Wolf River House resort and Lang's Landing, both in Winneconne, offer boat rentals.

The walleye population in the lakes is healthy.

"Right now we have a very robust population of medium-sized walleyes," Kamke said. "There are a lot of fish in that 16- to 20-inch range." Occasionally, people catch trophy walleyes in the eight- to ten-pound range, he said.

Coats, Butters and I launched at the Winneconne village ramp and motored across the lake to Clark's Bay on the north side.

There, we put out six medium-action trolling rods with line-counter reels and ten-pound-test monofilament. We ran an assortment of three-inch crank baits behind planer boards, from 2 to 2½ feet off the bottom in 4½ to 8 feet of water.

"The walleyes are done spawning," Coats said. "They're going into the bay with the warm water to feed on the bait fish-emerald shiners and shad. The northerns and white bass are there, too, for the bait fish."

Coats was right.

We fished all morning and part of the afternoon, finding most of our action in about $7\frac{1}{2}$ feet of water. We caught four walleyes, 17, 19 and 20 inches long, plus one small one; two northern pike, about 25 or 26 inches long; and a dozen or more white bass and sheepshead. We released everything but the three big walleyes, which met their destiny in a frying pan.

There is no size limit for walleyes on the lakes, and the daily bag limit is five. The bag limit for northerns is two, with a minimum length of 26 inches. The northern pike season is closed from March 1 until the first Saturday in May.

We experienced some good walleye action. But Coats said it will get even better as the water temperature, which was 48 degrees that day, warms up a bit.

"It wasn't quite warm enough yet," he said. "When the water temperature hits 52 or 53 degrees, the walleyes will get more aggressive."

LAKE KOSHKONONG/JEFFERSON COUNTY

FISH PRESENT

- Walleyes
- Saugers
- White Bass
- Largemouth Bass
- Smallmouth Bass
- Northern Pike
- Muskies
- Catfish
- Black Crappies
- Perch
- Bluegills

LAKE KOSHKONONG LORE:

"You never know what's at the end of your line. But every once in a while, you'll catch a nice walleye."
— Gary Wroblewski, guide

Acreage: **10,460**

Max. depth: **7** feet

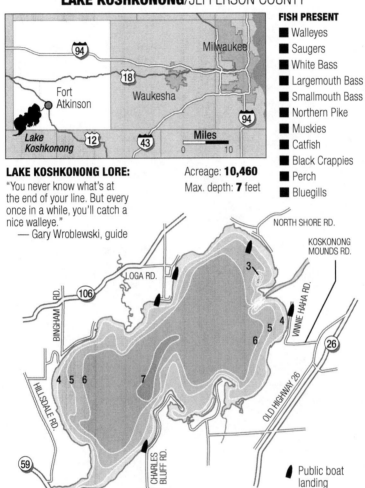

Public boat landing

Lake Koshkonong

FORT ATKINSON—If you're looking for some good walleye action, try Lake Koshkonong.

"The reality is that walleye fishing in southern Wisconsin can be tough," said Gary Wroblewski, a guide who has fished Koshkonong for ten years. "This is a lake where you can catch walleyes. You're going to catch other fish, too. You never know what's at the end of your line. But every once in a while, you'll catch a nice walleye."

Lake Koshkonong is a 10,460-acre lake in southwestern Jefferson County, with a maximum depth of just seven feet.

According to Don Bush with the DNR, Koshkonong was transformed from a deep-water marsh to a big, shallow lake by the Indianford dam on the Rock River, which was completed in 1917.

"Walleye is probably the most highly sought-after fish," Bush said.

The state stocks walleyes in Koshkonong to supplement a natural population. "We estimate that about 25 percent of the walleye fishery is stocked and 75 percent is natural," Bush said.

Koshkonong has had a carp problem for decades, and stocking of game fish is tied to carp removal. Private contractors, supervised by the DNR, take an average of about two million pounds of carp out of the lake each year.

Carp get into the lake from the Rock River, which flows through Koshkonong. Game fish and panfish are stocked to prey on carp and occupy the habitat they would otherwise use.

"The lake, itself, is prime habitat for carp—big and shallow with a muddy bottom and abundant lake fly larvae," Bush said. "That food is also the bread and butter for walleyes, catfish, panfish and white bass."

Typically, the lake gets about three million walleye fry a year but, this year, five hundred thousand one-inch walleye fingerlings were stocked. "We've had enormous success with fry stocking," Bush said. "We're trying to get a cost-benefit analysis of the fingerlings."

The DNR has reestablished a sauger population and is trying to do the same with yellow perch and flathead catfish. The state also stocks between

Gary Wroblewski shows off a walleye he caught while trolling
Lake Koshkonong.

five hundred thousand and two million northern pike fry a year to supplement a natural population, plus about 2,500 muskies.

In addition, the lake has naturally reproducing populations of white bass, largemouth bass, some smallmouth bass, channel catfish, bullheads, black crappies and bluegills.

Watersport Boat Rental, 723 E. Ellendale Road, Town of Newville, has two fishing boats with outboards for $65 a half-day or $85 a day, plus tax and gas. A $200 credit card security deposit is required.

Major boat landings are located off Charlie Bluff Road on the southwest side of the lake, Keuhn and Carcajou Roads on the north, North Shore Road on the northeast and Vinnie Haha Road on the southeast.

"If people have large boats, they're probably better off launching in the river," Bush advised. The DNR has free launches on the Rock River, off Groeler Road under the Highway 26 bypass, east of the lake; and about a mile downstream from I-90 in Newville, southwest of the lake.

Wroblewski, Larry Awe, and I paid $4 to launch at the Riverfront tavern on Blackhawk Island—one of several additional private landings—and motored out to mid-lake on a cloudy June evening with shifting winds and weather fronts moving through.

"Koshkonong is almost always better when it's windy," Wroblewski said. "I think wind increases the feeding activity."

Don't look for any sharp drop-offs, rock bars or other major structure.

"The lake is pretty much a big flat, so you look for changes from muck to sand bottom and subtle differences in depth," Wroblewski explained. "A foot or two change in depth can make the difference."

We set up four trolling rods with line-counter reels and eight-pound monofilament line, and tied on three-inch crank baits, which we set 10 to 12 feet behind planer boards dragged 25 to 35 yards behind the boat.

We trolled at about two miles per hour and, for the next five hours, had steady action reeling in a mixed bag of fish. We caught about 25 white bass, two northerns, a bullhead, two saugers and about a dozen walleyes, up to almost 19 inches long. We released everything but a couple of the walleyes, which we kept to eat.

"You'll likely catch more undersized walleyes than 'keepers,'" Bush said. "But Koshkonong can produce trophies. I've heard of several walleyes in the 27-inch range taken."

PIKE LAKE/WASHINGTON COUNTY

Miles

FISH PRESENT
- Walleyes
- Northern pike
- Largemouth bass
- Perch
- Bluegills
- Crappies

PIKE LAKE LORE:

"For size and numbers of walleyes, Pike Lake is as good as you'll find anywhere in southern Wisconsin, and it's probably even better than most northern lakes."
 – John Nelson, DNR

Acreage: **522**
Max. depth: **45** feet

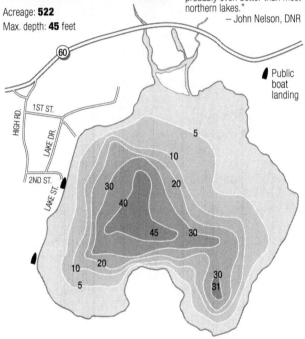

Public boat landing

Pike Lake

HARTFORD—We were hoping for some Pike Lake walleyes.
After all, that's what this lake in southwestern Washington County is mostly known for.

"For size and numbers of walleyes, Pike Lake is as good as you'll find anywhere in southern Wisconsin," said John Nelson of the DNR. "And it's probably even better than most northern lakes."

But when I spoke with Eric Skell, who lives on the lake, he had disappointing news. Skell, an avid walleye angler, had fished hard for several evenings and only caught one walleye.

"In July and August, it gets tough," he said.

We decided to try give it a try anyway, but with a back-up plan.

Pike Lake is a 522-acre lake with a maximum depth of 45 feet. There is a big mud flat on the north end and a good drop-off out from Eagle Point on the south.

"It has such a good naturally reproducing walleye population that we just keep hands off," Nelson said. "It hasn't been stocked with walleyes since around 1960."

In 2001, Nelson said, the Pike Lake Sportsman's Club and Walleyes for Tomorrow teamed up for a walleye spawning habitat improvement project by installing baseball size rubble along the shore at Eagle Point.

A DNR survey conducted in spring of 2000 found walleyes up to 23 inches long.

"The peak numbers were at 16 and 17 inches, but there were quite a few at 18 and 19 inches," Nelson said. "Most of these walleyes are going to be legal fish."

The boat launch at Reef Point Resort, 3416 Lake Drive, costs $7; and the one at Johnny's Landing, 3298 High Road, costs $6. Reef Point rents rowboats for $12 a day, boats with motors for $45, and pontoon boats for $145. Johnny's has rowboats for $7, and boats with motors for $30.

Skell said the best walleye fishing was in spring and fall, but he can usually pick up a fish or two in summer by trolling the deep weed edges at dusk.

Eric Skell shows off a bluegill from Pike Lake near Hartford.

Pike Lake is pretty with lots of natural, undeveloped shoreline. A state park along the eastern shore provides tree-lined scenery, plus access for shore anglers.

"Some people wade in, south of the swimming beach, and pick up walleyes at night," Nelson said.

In addition to walleyes, the DNR survey found largemouth bass, bluegills, crappies—plus perch up to nine inches and northern pike up to 29 1/2 inches long.

The lake gets a lot of ice fishing pressure.

"I really expected to see bigger perch [in the survey]," Nelson said. "I think they get some nice ones in deep water through the ice. The lake doesn't have a lot of northerns, but it will produce an occasional 20-pound-plus fish through the ice."

When I met up with Skell and Terry Schuler, of West Bend, one August afternoon, we decided to start out drift-fishing for suspended bluegills that move out to the cool, deep water in late summer.

We boarded Skell's boat and motored to the east shore where we set up and drifted west with the wind over 18 to 25 feet of water, then motored back and drifted out again.

"There's a huge number of bluegills in this lake," Skell said.

I used an ultralight slip-bobber rig, while Skell and Schuler each went with a "Mendota rig," a long tubular weight rigged above a short monofilament leader. We all used a 1/32-ounce jig tipped with either a wax worm or a piece of night crawler.

Both caught fish. Most of our bites came near the bottom, 12 to 18 feet down, a situation that Skell attributed to presence of water skiers in the area.

"Boat traffic pushes the fish to the bottom," he said. "The fish will come up when the activity dies down."

Even so, in less than three hours, we picked up a dozen nice panfish: 11 bluegills, up to about nine inches, plus one crappie.

An hour or so before sundown, we decided to switch to trolling four-inch crank baits on planer boards for those elusive walleyes, but we couldn't find any takers.

"You'll have to come back for the walleyes in the fall," Skell said.

Sounds like a good plan to me.

Panfish

J. Riepenhoff

Panfish

J.Riepenhoff

For those of us who love to fish, it probably all began with a bouncing bobber and a panfish on the end of the line. Bluegills, crappies, perch, sunfish and rock bass are abundant in southern Wisconsin waters, and they are easy to catch.

What they lack in size, panfish make up for in numbers. Pound for pound, they provide more pure fishing pleasure to more anglers than bigger, more prestigious game fish. And, of course, they are called panfish, because, pan-fried, they make excellent table fare.

The panfish season remains open all year on most lakes, so the fun never ends. You can catch them through the ice and in open water, as soon as the ice is out.

A small piece of live bait—a wax worm, leaf worm, a few spikes or a piece of night crawler—hooked onto a small ice jig or a plain hook beneath a bobber on ultralight spinning gear is generally all it takes. Small plastic lures can also be effective. Crappies sometimes prefer a small minnow on a number eight hook.

Panfish are among the first fish of spring. After ice-out, typically in early April, look for them in the shallow bays and channels, in about six to ten feet of water, on the north side of the lakes, because those areas warm up first.

Panfish spawn in the shallow water. Some, especially bluegills, continue to use the shoreline shallows all summer long. Wear glare-cutting sunglasses and you will see them in the shady water beneath piers or overhanging branches.

Larger panfish can be found in a little deeper water, near weeds. We found some nice-sized perch on Lake Monona fishing underwater weed humps in summer.

For a real treat, try using a fly rod to cast a small popper or wet fly over the weed beds and hang on. Landing a feisty bluegill or crappie on a fly rod will make you fall in love with panfishing all over again.

In mid- to late summer, many anglers like to drift over deep water with their bait down 15 feet or more for suspended panfish. Look for clusters of fish on your locater. Slip-bobber rigs, which make it easy to cast and adjust the depth of your bait presentation, work well for this technique. Monona, Mendota, Rock, Delavan and Nagawicka are all good lakes to fish for suspended panfish.

Another effective method is using a "loaded" rod. Tie a heavy weight, a half-ounce or more with swivels on either end, to the line and a 12- to 16-inch leader above the bait. The weight puts a bend in the rod and, when you fish straight down, makes the slightest bite easy to detect.

In fall and winter, look for panfish near green weeds that produce oxygen in 5 to 12 feet of water, although crappies and perch sometimes suspend over deep water.

All lakes have panfish. Some of the better ones are profiled in this chapter.

DELAVAN LAKE/WALWORTH COUNTY

DELAVAN LAKE LORE:

"I caught two of the biggest bluegills of my life out of Delavan Lake back in the late 1980s. They measured $10^{1}/_{4}$ inches and weighed over a pound."

– Jim Laganowski, guide

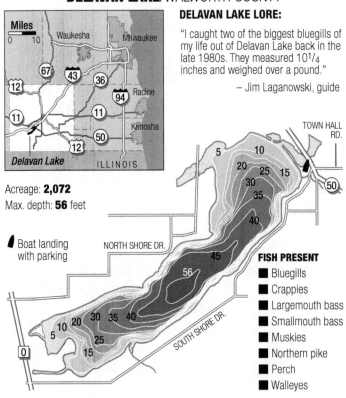

Acreage: **2,072**
Max. depth: **56** feet

◢ Boat landing with parking

FISH PRESENT

■ Bluegills
■ Crappies
■ Largemouth bass
■ Smallmouth bass
■ Muskies
■ Northern pike
■ Perch
■ Walleyes

Delavan Lake

DELAVAN—Delavan Lake is known for producing big panfish.
"I caught two of the biggest bluegills of my life out of Delavan Lake back in the late 1980s," said Jim Laganowski, a guide who has fished the lake for more than 20 years. "They measured 10 ¼ inches and weighed over a pound."

And Doug Welch of the DNR said this: "In the early and mid-1990s, they were catching bluegills up to 12 inches long."

Delavan Lake has the right food supply to produce slab panfish, Welch explained.

"It's a real fertile lake," he said. "It produces a lot of aquatic insects and invertebrates that bluegills and other panfish feed on."

Located in central Walworth County, Delavan is a 2,072-acre lake with a maximum depth of 56 feet.

In 1990 and 1991, the lake underwent a major DNR carp eradication and game fish restoration project. Now it's one of the more productive and heavily fished lakes in southeastern Wisconsin, drawing anglers from Milwaukee, Madison, Janesville, Beloit and Chicago.

A "Mixed Bag"

Fishing reopened on Delavan Lake in 1992 with special regulations established to protect the new fishery. The regulations call for a 40-inch minimum length and a daily bag limit of one musky; a 32-inch length and a daily bag of one northern pike; an 18-inch length and a daily bag of one bass, either a largemouth or a smallmouth; and a minimum length of 18 inches and a daily bag of three walleyes.

"It's a mixed bag," Welch said. "People fish for all kinds of fish."

The DNR's 2003 quotas call for stocking 2,500 muskies eight to ten inches long, about five hundred thousand walleye fry, and 51,800 smallmouth bass fingerlings.

Guide Jim Laganowski admires a big crappie from Delavan Lake in Walworth County.

In addition, Welch said, the lake has naturally reproducing populations of largemouth bass, northern pike and panfish, including bluegills, crappies, sunfish and yellow perch.

A DNR fish survey in spring of 2003 showed "good numbers of northern pike up to 38 inches, largemouth bass up to 21 inches and a few smallmouths up to about 18 inches," Welch said.

"There were lots of walleyes out there, good numbers of females between 16 and 24 inches long," he said. "Most males were between 13 and 18 inches long."

The survey turned up just three muskies, the biggest of which was 43 inches long and weighed 24 pounds.

"The muskies aren't that abundant," Welch said. "But the muskies that are there grow well."

Welch is considering switching to stocking larger muskies, from 12 to 18 inches long, to try and improve their chances of surviving predation by northerns, bass and walleyes.

The survey also showed lots of small yellow perch, indicating that perch fishing will be very good in future years.

The Town of Delavan operates a public boat landing off Highway 50 on the east end of the lake. The cost is $7.

Gordy's Marina rents boats at Lake Lawn Lodge, 2400 Geneva Road, from Memorial Day through Labor Day. They have one aluminum boat with an outboard for $30 per hour or $85 for four hours, plus gas. They also rent 18-foot runabouts to fishermen, when available, for $125 for four hours. Geneva Lake Bait and Tackle, located three-tenths of a mile south of Highway 50 on Highway 67, also rents fishing boats "by appointment" for $60 a day.

"We have to drop the boat off and pick it up at a fixed time, unless they have their own hitch," said Brian Gates, who operates the bait shop.

When Laganowski and I visited Delavan Lake one May afternoon, we were looking for big panfish. We launched our boat, motored past the long rock rubble peninsula that shelters the launch site—and also provides plenty of access for shore anglers—and anchored at our first spot, a submerged weed bed in about seven feet of water.

Change of Tactics

We used ultralight spinning gear with four-pound monofilament to suspend a wax worm hooked on a small chicken-feather jig a few feet beneath a slip bobber.

The action was slow. We tried a few different spots, picking up a few bluegills up to about eight inches long, here and there, before finding our most consistent action in the shallow bay on the north end of the lake.

About an hour before sundown, we decided to switch locations and try for crappies. We joined a couple other boats anchored along an outside weed line in about 12 feet of water, and used the same slip-bobber rigs to suspend small minnows instead of wax worms.

For the next hour or so, before the wind shifted from west to north, we had steady action with some very big crappies, up to 12 or 13 inches long. We released some, and kept a few for a fish fry.

"We didn't get the big bluegills that Delavan Lake is noted for," Laganowski said afterward. "But we got the big crappies."

UPPER/LOWER PHANTOM LAKES/WAUKESHA COUNTY

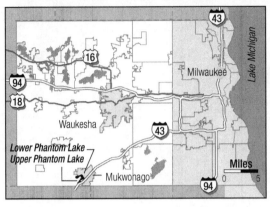

Lower Phantom Lake

Acreage: **433**
Max. depth: **12** feet

FISH PRESENT

- Northern pike
- Walleyes
- Largemouth bass
- Catfish
- Crappies
- Bluegills
- Pumpkinseeds
- Bullheads

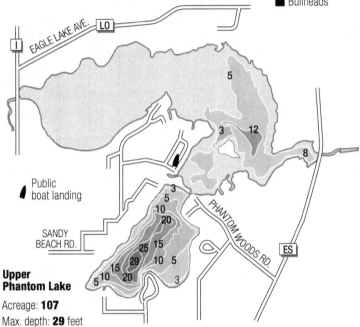

Public boat landing

Upper Phantom Lake

Acreage: **107**
Max. depth: **29** feet

FISH PRESENT

- Northern pike
- Walleyes
- Largemouth bass
- Smallmouth bass
- Bluegills
- Crappies
- Perch
- Rock bass
- Sunfish

LOWER PHANTOM LAKE LORE:

"Most of Lower Phantom is marshy and hard to get a boat through."
— Sue Beyler, DNR

Upper and Lower Phantom Lakes

MUKWONAGO—As the boat drifted silently into the shoreline shallows, I worked my fly line out in a backward loop, then cast it forward to gently drop a yellow "popper" on the surface of some shady water next to a pier.

It didn't take long for a big bluegill to come up and suck it in. When it did, I lifted the rod tip to set the hook and began stripping in line.

For its size, the bluegill put up an impressive fight, as they always do on a fly rod. Using its stout little body, the feisty 'gill made a dash for the weeds and spun around in circles before I could hoist it into the boat.

The scene took place one hot, sunny July morning on Upper Phantom Lake, when the breeze was mild enough to cool you off a little and let you to cast a fly line.

I was fishing with Larry Awe, who was busy using his own favorite pan-fish method. He hooked a piece of night crawler on a jig suspended a foot or so beneath a bobber using ultralight spinning gear.

"I use a flu-flu jig," Awe explained. "It has a small cluster of chicken feathers tied to a $\frac{1}{64}$-ounce jig. The feathers are what does it. They hold the scent of the night crawler."

Successful Day

Both methods proved to be very effective that morning. We worked the dark water near piers, pontoon boats and overhanging trees. It didn't take long to catch enough bluegills for a fish fry, and we still had time left over to do some largemouth bass fishing.

Lower Phantom Lake is a 433-acre lake with a maximum depth of 12 feet, while Upper Phantom Lake, to the south, has another 107 acres with a maximum depth of 29 feet.

127

Larry Awe releases a largemouth bass on Upper Phantom Lake, which is located near Mukwonago. Bluegills are also plentiful on the lake.

There is a free public launch in a village park off Andrews Street, in Mukwonago, on the south side of Lower Phantom Lake.

I have fished the Phantoms for years, spending most of my time on Upper Phantom in pursuit of either largemouth bass or bluegills.

"Most of Lower Phantom is marshy and hard to get a boat through," said Sue Beyler of the DNR. But Upper Phantom Lake has clear water and a defined, visible weed line that can hold lots of fish.

To supplement a natural population, the DNR stocks about 2,165 six- to eight-inch northern pike fingerlings every year. And, in an effort to establish a walleye population, the state has been stocking walleyes since the late 1990s with more than 50,000 two-inch walleye fingerling every other year.

The DNR is conducting a study of its walleyes stocking methods.

"The Phantom lakes are part of a study to compare the stocking of two-inch fingerlings with extended-growth walleyes that are five to six inches long," Beyler said.

The Phantom lakes are getting about 5,400 extended-growth walleyes, while four other lakes get the smaller, traditional fingerlings. DNR crews will go back and take samples to see how many of each type survived.

"We're trying to see if we get more bang for our buck by stocking fewer big fish or many small ones," Beyler explained.

Wide Variety

The Phantoms also have natural populations of largemouth bass, bluegills, crappies, perch, sunfish and bullheads.

While walleye fishing is picking up, Beyler said: "Summer anglers are mainly after bass, and ice fishermen mainly fish for northerns and panfish."

In winter, fishing pressure can be extreme. "There are so many shanties that Lower Phantom looks like a town out on the ice," Beyler said.

But on a hot summer week day, the Phantoms can be a quiet, peaceful place to fish.

That's what Awe and I found when we launched the boat and motored south through the narrows that leads to Upper Phantom Lake.

In addition to the bluegills, we caught several largemouth bass that morning.

In the past, I've taken some nice-sized, late-summer largemouths by "slop fishing" weedless plastic frogs over the top of the thick weeds near the Mukwonago River outlet on the east end of Lower Phantom.

This time, Awe and I concentrated our efforts on the inside weed line and the south and west shores of Upper Phantom Lake. We both tied pre-rigged plastic worms on to medium-action spinning gear, strung with eight-pound monofilament line and started casting.

That was all we really had to do to get some pretty good bass action.

We caught and released seven or eight largemouths that morning, up to about 13 inches long. "I'd like to come back sometime and try it again real early in the morning for bigger bass," Awe said.

There's a plan might be worth a try.

LITTLE GREEN LAKE/GREEN LAKE COUNTY

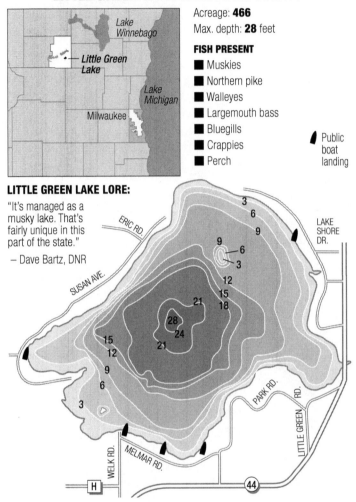

Acreage: **466**
Max. depth: **28** feet

FISH PRESENT

■ Muskies
■ Northern pike
■ Walleyes
■ Largemouth bass
■ Bluegills
■ Crappies
■ Perch

◢ Public boat landing

LITTLE GREEN LAKE LORE:

"It's managed as a musky lake. That's fairly unique in this part of the state."

– Dave Bartz, DNR

Lake Winnebago

Little Green Lake

Lake Michigan

Milwaukee

ERIC RD.

SUSAN AVE.

LAKE SHORE DR.

PARK RD.

LITTLE GREEN RD.

WELK RD.

MELMAR RD.

H

44

Little Green Lake

MARKESAN—Little Green Lake has a big reputation for muskies. "It's managed as a musky lake," said Dave Bartz of the DNR. "That's fairly unique in this part of the state."

The lake has become a central Wisconsin destination for musky anglers, and with good reason.

According to the musky board posted at The Landing, a boat launch and tackle shop located on the south side of lake, Little Green Lake anglers registered 45 legal muskies in 2002, up to 49 ½ inches long, through late September.

"There were two 49 ½-inchers," said Tom Munsey, who operates The Landing. "One was kept and one was released."

Both size and number were improvements over 2001, when anglers registered 30 muskies all year, and the biggest one measured 48 inches.

Little Green is a 466-acre lake with a maximum depth of 28 feet. Back in 1957, the lake was poisoned for carp eradication and, after that, the DNR started stocking muskies.

"The state quota calls for stocking 932 10- or 11-inch true muskies a year," Bartz said. "Also, the Portage Musky Club has provided about 500 tiger muskies a year in recent years."

In addition to muskies, Little Green Lake has good panfish and bass fishing. The lake has self-sustaining populations of largemouth bass, bluegills, crappies, perch and northern pike.

Stocked walleyes also get a fair amount of angler attention. The DNR stocks 23,000 walleye fingerlings every other year.

When I met up with Randy Butters and Bret Hennig, both of Ripon, at Muncey's boat launch, we planned to spend the morning in pursuit of muskies.

The Landing, at W2138 Melmar Drive, charges $2 to launch a boat. It has 14-foot aluminum rowboats for rent at $15 a day, or a boat with a six-horsepower outboard for $45. Bigger outboards, a fully equipped fishing boat and a pontoon boat are all available for more money.

Randy Butters unhooks a crappie from his line on Little Green Lake. The lake is known for muskies but also has a variety of panfish.

Easy Access

There are public launches located on Kearley's Bay off Highway O on the west end; off Lake Shore Drive on the northeast side; and off Welk Road on the south, although this one has limited parking and is used mainly by ice fishermen in winter, Bartz said. Vandy's Lakeshore Pub also operates a launch on the southeast end.

Little Green is a fairly easy lake to fish. We used an electric trolling motor to work our way along the shoreline, using heavy bait-casting tackle to throw surface lures, jerk baits or bucktails along the outside weed line in 6 to 12 feet of water. We fished the steep drop-offs along the southeast and northeast shores, and the big weed bed on the east end.

Hennig showed us the place where he caught and released a 44-inch musky in June of 2001, and I pointed out the spot where I did the same with a 30-incher back in 1995. You don't forget the places where you catch a musky—any musky.

This time, though, the muskies didn't cooperate. After about three hours of casting big lures, we hadn't even seen a musky follow.

"You wouldn't see them anyway with all this algae," Butters observed. "The water is too green."

Maybe that's where the lake got its name.

At any rate, after a lunch break, we decided to try for some panfish.

Bluegills Plentiful

"The majority of people fish for panfish," Munsey said. "There's an abundance of bluegills in this lake. The crappies are kind of hit-and-miss, but the bluegills are always available."

We caught both, using a bottom-fishing technique that Butters demonstrated.

We found panfish on the locater, clustered near the bottom in 12 to 16 feet of water, and anchored the boat. We made slip-sinker rigs by sliding a $^{1}/_{8}$-ounce egg sinker onto four- or six-pound mono, squeezing a tiny split-shot on the line below the egg sinker to make a 6- to 12-inch leader. We tied small panfish hooks to the leaders, dressed them with either a leaf worm or a piece of night crawler, cast out and slowly dragged the bait back.

"When you drag the egg sinker across the bottom, the reeling action makes the bait float up off the bottom," Butters explained. "It also creates a disturbance, little puffs of silt that attract the fish."

In a few hours, we caught more than 20 bluegills and crappies, up to about nine inches long. We kept a few big ones, and threw the others back.

We didn't get the thrill of catching a big musky, but all those panfish added up to a fine afternoon.

EAGLE LAKE/RACINE COUNTY

Miles
0   5

WAUKESHA COUNTY
(83)
(36)
MILWAUKEE COUNTY
Milwaukee

Eagle Lake
(45)
Racine
(20)
(11)

Town of Dover

Lake Michigan

KENOSHA COUNTY

Burlington
(75)
(94)

Acreage: **515**
Max. depth: **12** feet

EAGLE LAKE LORE:

"Eagle Lake is one of the few lakes I know of in southeastern Wisconsin that has an ice-out panfish bite."

– Jim Laganowski, fisherman

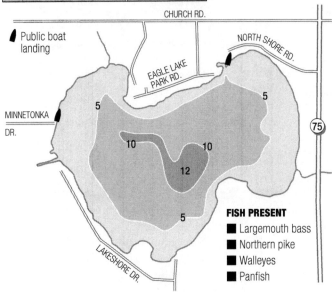

CHURCH RD.

NORTH SHORE RD.

▸ Public boat landing

EAGLE LAKE PARK RD.

MINNETONKA DR.

(75)

5
5
10
10
12
5

LAKESHORE DR.

FISH PRESENT
■ Largemouth bass
■ Northern pike
■ Walleyes
■ Panfish

Eagle Lake

KANSASVILLE—When we drove up to the boat landing at Eagle Lake one rainy April morning, the shoreline was packed with anglers.

"Eagle Lake is one of the few lakes I know of in southeastern Wisconsin that has an ice-out panfish bite," Jim Laganowski told me.

And, judging by the crowd, the bite was on.

Eagle Lake is a 515-acre lake with a maximum depth of 12 feet, located in central Racine County.

In 1991, sport fishing had all but vanished in the lake because of an infestation of carp and bullheads. The problem was so severe that the DNR decided the best solution was to kill every fish in the lake and start over.

Sport fishing reopened in 1995, after a $150,000 rough fish eradication and game fish restoration project.

Today, the lake has self-sustaining populations of largemouth bass, crappies, bluegills, sunfish and yellow perch. In addition, the DNR stocks about 25,000 two- to three-inch walleye fingerlings and 2,500 six- to eight-inch northern pike every other year.

Special regulations set a daily bag limit of one largemouth bass, which must be 18 inches or longer; and a total daily panfish bag limit of 15 fish.

Good Bass Fishing

"It's one of our best largemouth bass lakes," said Doug Welch of the DNR. "There are a lot of nice-sized fish there approaching 17 and 18 inches. If you like to fish for above-average size largemouth bass and get a lot of action, that would be the place to go."

There are two public launches, one at Eagle Lake Park, off Church Road on the north side of the lake, and another off Minnetonka Drive on the west side. The cost is $5. There are no boat rentals.

Anglers like to cast the north shoreline shallows for bass, anchor off the point on the northwest side to fish for perch, or jig along an underwater gravel bar that juts out from the south side for walleyes, Welch said. Most northerns are taken through the ice in winter by tip-up anglers, he said.

Anglers line the shore of the boat launch on the north side of Eagle Lake on a rainy morning.

For our trip, a unique, seasonal panfish opportunity brought us to Eagle Lake for some ice-out shoreline fishing.

Laganowski has been fishing the ice-out bite for the past few years.

"It's the first open water panfish bite of the year," he explained. "It starts about a week after ice-out and lasts for two to three weeks."

In general, after ice-out, fish seek the warmest water in the lake, which is always on the north side because it gets the most sun.

"The shallow water and black lake bottom also help this area warm up first," Laganowski said. "That's what attracts the panfish."

In early spring, the water in Eagle Lake's boat launch channel area is "at least 5 degrees warmer than the lake proper," Welch said.

"It's warm," Laganowski said. "The fish are in there feeding after not eating much during the cold winter months under the ice."

There were about 25 or 30 anglers working the shoreline around the boat launch when we arrived.

Laganowski and I looked around for Ryan Machajewski, of Greendale, who was saving us a spot and had already caught several crappies, plus a few bluegills.

We used ultra-light spinning gear with light line and a slip-bobber rig to suspend a $\frac{1}{16}$-ounce jig dressed with a wax worm about a foot and half beneath the bobber.

Attention Required

All you had to do was cast out and keep a close eye on your bobber. It didn't always go under when you got a bite. Sometimes a crappie would move it to the side a little, or just stop its drift. So you had to pay attention.

But the action was phenomenal.

We fished through a morning rain that nobody seemed to care about because we were too busy catching fish. We threw back the small ones and put the fish big enough to fillet in our buckets.

"What you don't catch in size, you make up for in quantity," Laganowski said.

After about three and a half hours of constant action, we each had enough panfish—mostly crappies, but also a few bluegills and sunfish—to bring home for a fish fry.

So we decided to call it a day. But you can bet that I'll be back for more of this ice-out panfishing next year.

ROCK LAKE/JEFFERSON COUNTY

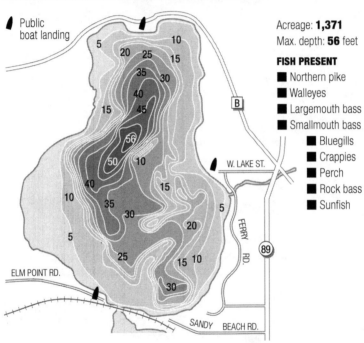

Public boat landing

Acreage: **1,371**

Max. depth: **56** feet

FISH PRESENT

■ Northern pike
■ Walleyes
■ Largemouth bass
■ Smallmouth bass
■ Bluegills
■ Crappies
■ Perch
■ Rock bass
■ Sunfish

Rock Lake

L AKE MILLS—When fishing, it's always a good idea to pay attention
to details.

There's the water temperature, the depth, the rocks, the weeds
and other structure, the bait and the tackle. And while you're at it, don't forget to keep an eye on the anglers in the other boats to see what they're
doing.

That last method, although not exactly scientific, can be the very productive. In fact, it saved the day on a recent trip to Rock Lake in Jefferson
County.

Gary Wroblewski and I had our hearts set on catching a few smallmouth
bass.

"It's one of the best smallmouth bass lakes in southern Wisconsin," said
Wroblewski, who has been fishing Rock Lake for 20 years.

Rock Lake is a 1,371-acre lake, with maximum depth of 56 feet.

"The thing I like about Rock Lake is that it has the characteristics of a
northern Wisconsin lake," Wroblewski told me. "It has clear water, rocky
shorelines and reefs, and defined weed beds—all of which make it an interesting lake to fish."

Pyramids Add to Structure

According to Laura Stremick-Thompson, fisheries biologist with the
Department of Natural Resources at Horicon, Rock Lake also has a unique
series of underwater pyramid-like structures.

"There is a lot of speculation that these pyramids are relics from a prior
civilization," Stremick-Thompson said. "There have been books written
about it."

While they may be fascinating to divers and archeologists, from a fishing standpoint, the pyramids are just one more type of structure in a lake
that is abundant with structure.

The Town of Lake Mills operates a public boat landing off Highway B on
the north end of the lake that costs $3. The city operates two—one that

Gary Wroblewski shows off one of the nice-sized bluegills taken just before sunset on an expedition to Rock Lake in Jefferson County.

costs $4 for state residents and $6 for non-residents at Sandy Beach on the southeast side, and a free landing on the mill pond on the east side. Since you have to go beneath a culvert to access the lake form the mill pond landing, it isn't suitable for large boats. There are no boat rentals.

According to Stremick-Thompson, Rock Lake has natural populations of both largemouth and smallmouth bass. "Most people fish it for bass," she said.

There are also naturally reproducing populations of northern pike, bluegills, crappies, perch, rock bass and sunfish. The DNR occasionally stocks northern pike to supplement the natural population. In 1999, one hundred thousand northern pike fry were stocked.

The DNR also stocks walleyes.

"Rock Lake is not a natural walleye lake," Stremick-Thompson said. "But there is a lot of interest in attempting to make it a walleye lake."

After stocking walleye fry for years, the DNR recently switched to stocking larger, extended-growth walleyes that are six to seven inches long in hopes of getting better survival rates. In 2001, 11,000 extended-growth walleyes were stocked.

In addition, Stremick-Thompson said: "Because of its proximity to our Lake Mills fish hatchery, whenever they have extra fish—northerns or walleyes—that (Rock Lake) is where they get stocked."

A fish survey conducted in 2000 and 2001 showed largemouth bass up to 17½ inches long, smallmouth bass up to 17 inches, northerns up to 40 inches, walleyes up to 25½ inches, and bluegills up to about 9 inches.

"A lot of the bluegills were in the eight- and nine-inch range," Stremick-Thompson said. "You can usually go out there and get good-sized panfish year after year."

That's what Wroblewski and I ended up doing one July evening.

Slow Start, Late Rally

We started out by casting suspending minnow baits over a few rock and sand reefs in pursuit of smallmouth bass. But after a couple hours, we only managed to catch one small one.

"The smallmouth bass fishing is best early in the spring," Wroblewski said.

So we switched to working the deep weed line with night crawlers, a method that has produced both bass and walleyes for Wroblewski in the past. This time, however, we only caught one largemouth bass.

The sun was just about ready to set when we noticed a boat with two guys in it. They were both busy reeling in bluegill after bluegill.

So we motored over to horn in on their party, doing our best to keep our boat a polite distance away.

The anglers were anchored in about ten feet of water, but they were right on the break line, so their bait, a cast away, was probably in 18 to 20 feet.

We anchored and set up slip-bobber rigs to suspend a piece of night crawler 9 to 11 feet down, just above the deep weeds, and, before long, started catching some nice-sized bluegills of our own. The biggest ones were up to about nine inches long.

"Rock Lake has always had a reputation for producing big bluegills," Wroblewski said. "It's one of my favorite southern Wisconsin lakes."

FOX LAKE/DODGE COUNTY

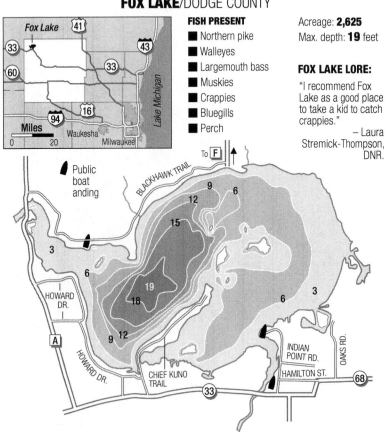

FISH PRESENT
- Northern pike
- Walleyes
- Largemouth bass
- Muskies
- Crappies
- Bluegills
- Perch

Acreage: **2,625**
Max. depth: **19** feet

FOX LAKE LORE:

"I recommend Fox Lake as a good place to take a kid to catch crappies."
– Laura Stremick-Thompson, DNR.

Fox Lake

FOX LAKE—If you like to catch crappies, consider Fox Lake.

"Fox Lake is a crappie lake," according to Laura Stremick-Thompson of the DNR. "They're not exceptionally huge fish, but they're healthy, they're fat and there are lots of them."

And they are fun to catch.

Jim Laganowski and I found that out one February day, on the snow-covered frozen surface of the lake, where we caught a mixed-bag of panfish, made up mostly of crappies.

Fox Lake is a 2,625-acre lake, located in northwest Dodge County, about an hour and half drive from Milwaukee.

"Half of it is a shallow impoundment and the other half is a deeper lake," Stremick-Thompson said.

There are public boat landings in the Mill Creek outlet at Clauser Park, off Hamilton St. on the southeast side of the lake; and in Town Park, off Blackhawk Trail on the northwest side. The cost is $2.

Fish 'N' Fun Resort, W1599 Blackhawk Trail, has a free launch and rents rowboats for $15, boats and motors for $35, and pontoon boats for $135. Hayes Resort, W10551 Blackhawk Trail, rents rowboats for $8, and boats and motors for $35. And Indian Point Lodge, W10213 Indian Point Road, rents rowboats for $10, boats and motors for $30, and you can use their launch for "a donation."

Trouble Times

The lake has a history of water-quality problems caused by carp. In 1997, the DNR conducted a yearlong draw-down aimed at enhancing the growth of aquatic vegetation needed for fish habitat. During the draw-down, game fish and panfish survived in the deep holes on the west end, and more were stocked when water levels were restored.

"Unfortunately, that was one of the wettest summers on record," Stremick-Thompson said. "We didn't get the full draw-down effect. Overall, water clarity did not improve the way we hoped."

Jim Laganowski shows a mixed bag of crappies, bluegills and perch caught through the ice on Fox Lake.

And, for the most part, neither did the fishery.

"There is a fairly good northern pike population, but the population is smaller than it has been historically," Stremick-Thompson said. "Walleyes are the about same, although there has been some improvement."

The DNR stocks 2.6 million northern pike fingerlings and 130,000 walleye fingerlings a year. Musky stocking, which dated to the mid-1980s, was discontinued after fall of 2002.

"There is concern that the muskies will compete with northern pike," Stremick-Thompson said. "I think there is the sentiment that the northerns are what typically used to be here in large numbers."

Special regulations set a 32-inch minimum length for northerns and a daily bag limit of one; and an 18-inch minimum length for walleyes with a daily bag of three.

"The idea is to try and build up the predator population for carp control," Stremick-Thompson said. The DNR also kills carp with spot chemical treatments each spring and commercial fishermen remove hundreds of thousands of pounds of carp each year.

Since 2000, the Fox Lake Property Owners Association has stocked up to 12,000 yellow perch a year. In addition, the lake has naturally reproducing populations of largemouth bass, bluegills and those ever-present crappies.

"The crappies seem to do well in turbid water," Stremick-Thompson explained. "I recommend Fox Lake as a good place to take a kid to catch crappies."

In spring and summer, anglers fish for crappies and other panfish around the cluster of islands off Kuno Point.

Laganowski and I found them beneath the February ice, scattered in about three to nine feet of water on the west end.

Good Fishing

We parked the truck at the Town Park launch and walked out about a half-mile or so, where we joined clusters of ice anglers. This was my first trip to Fox Lake, although Laganowski has fished it for years, both through the ice and in open water.

"Fox Lake has been one of the more productive ice fishing lakes around Milwaukee," said Laganowski. "It's been a consistent producer."

We used ultralight spinning rods with two-pound monofilament line on short jigging rods tipped with spring bobbers. We tied on tiny light-colored jigs and dressed them with a wax worm.

We didn't have to drill any holes because there were plenty leftover from the weekend fishermen. We kept on the move, picking up a fish or two here and there.

"It's called hole hopping," Laganowski said. "You move from hole to hole, catch an aggressive fish or two, then move on."

In about four hours, we caught close to 30 fish. We threw the little ones back.

NAGAWICKA LAKE/WAUKESHA COUNTY

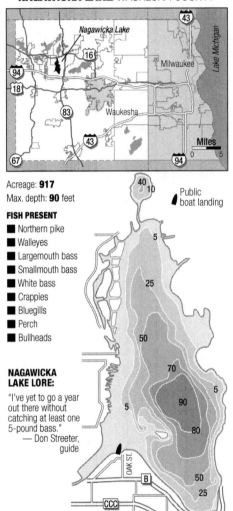

Acreage: **917**
Max. depth: **90** feet

FISH PRESENT

■ Northern pike
■ Walleyes
■ Largemouth bass
■ Smallmouth bass
■ White bass
■ Crappies
■ Bluegills
■ Perch
■ Bullheads

**NAGAWICKA
LAKE LORE:**

"I've yet to go a year
out there without
catching at least one
5-pound bass."
— Don Streeter,
guide

Public
boat landing

Nagawicka Lake

DELAFIELD—When Don Streeter skipped a plastic worm underneath a docked pontoon boat on Lake Nagawicka, I expected him to hook a largemouth bass, like I've seen him do so many times before.

This time, though, he surprised me, and maybe himself, by hooking a big bluegill.

"That one really slammed it," Streeter said, as he reeled in a 'gill that must have been eight or nine inches long.

Before that fish gave us a clue, we were having trouble finding active bluegills because of a July cold front that moved through overnight, dropping the air temperature from the nineties to the seventies.

"Typically, a cold front shuts fishing down or makes it more difficult," Streeter explained. "The fish get spooky. They're on guard more. You have to be quiet, make long casts and present the bait tight to cover."

Even on a good day, Nagawicka can be a tough lake to fish.

"It gets some of the heaviest fishing pressure in the state," said Sue Beyler of the DNR.

A survey done in 1985 and 1986 showed that Nagawicka ranked right behind Pewaukee Lake in terms of fishing pressure.

"For every acre in the lake, there was more than 30 hours of fishing," Beyler said.

Lake Nagawicka also gets heavy use by water skiers, jet skiers and sail boaters.

"If you want to fish it in summer, go early in the morning or in the evening to avoid the boat traffic," Beyler recommends.

Nagawicka is a 917-acre lake with a maximum depth of 90 feet. Waukesha County operates a public boat launch in Naga-Waukee Park, off Mariner Road on the east side of the lake. The cost is $5.25 on week days, and $6.75 weekends and holidays. There are no boat rentals.

Diverse Structure

Streeter, who has fished the lake for 26 years, likes the diversity of structure.

Although it is a heavily fished lake, Lake Nagawicka still has many big large-mouth bass and bluegills.

"It has rock bars and points, a sunken island, weed flats, 'The Kettle' basin on the north end, and stumps and lily pads," he said.

The DNR stocks 4,585 northern pike fingerlings every year, and 91,700 walleye fingerlings every other year.

"Both are supplements to naturally reproducing populations," Beyler said.

In addition, the lake has natural populations of largemouth and smallmouth bass, bluegills, perch, crappies, sunfish and bullheads.

Special regulations in effect since the mid-1980s prohibit any weed cutting, poisoning or dredging in three environmentally sensitive areas: The Kettle on the north end, the west side along the channels, and the southwest side in the outlet areas.

"These are the best areas for spawning, mainly for bass, panfish and minnows," Beyler said. "We've protected those areas and it has paid off."

A game fish survey in 1987 showed northern pike up to 41 inches, plus several largemouth bass 20 inches and longer.

Streeter caught the biggest bass of his life on this lake.

"I caught a 24-inch, 7½-pound largemouth bass on Nagawicka back in the late '80s or early '90s," he said. "I've yet to go a year out there without catching at least one five-pound bass."

A DNR panfish survey done in fall of 1999 showed crappies up to ten inches, perch up to nine inches and bluegills up to 8½ inches.

"The bluegills have plenty of spawning habitat and their growth rate is good," Beyler said. "You don't see stunted bluegills out there."

Once Streeter and I figured out that the bluegills were holding tight to cover, we went after them a little more slowly and methodically, and we did OK.

It Takes Work

We suspended a plastic grub or a live leech beneath a bobber on ultralight spinning gear, and made long casts next to piers, overhanging trees or weed lines.

"They're scattered," Streeter said. "This is not the time to anchor the boat and wait for fish to come to you. You have to go look for them."

So we kept moving and searching, picking up a fish or two here and there, and, after a few hours, we had enough bluegills for a fish fry.

"It's not the easiest lake to fish," Streeter said. "But if you take the time to learn it, it's a great lake."

WIND LAKE/RACINE COUNTY

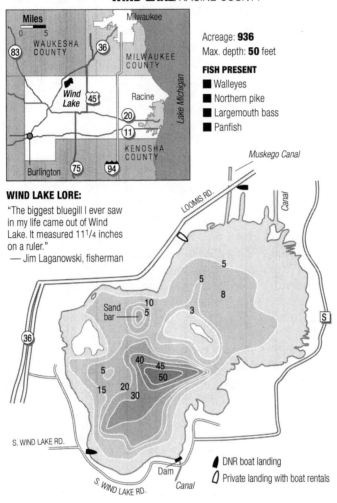

Acreage: **936**
Max. depth: **50** feet

FISH PRESENT
- Walleyes
- Northern pike
- Largemouth bass
- Panfish

WIND LAKE LORE:

"The biggest bluegill I ever saw in my life came out of Wind Lake. It measured 11 1/4 inches on a ruler."
— Jim Laganowski, fisherman

Milwaukee

WAUKESHA COUNTY

83

36

MILWAUKEE COUNTY

Wind Lake 45

Racine

Lake Michigan

20

11

KENOSHA COUNTY

Burlington 75 94

Miles
0 5

Muskego Canal

LOOMIS RD.

Canal

Sand bar

10
5

5

8

3

S

40 45
50

5

20
15 30

S. WIND LAKE RD.

Dam

S. WIND LAKE RD.

Canal

36

DNR boat landing

Private landing with boat rentals

Wind Lake

WIND LAKE—Midsummer can be a tough time to catch fish, but it's never impossible.

On a July visit to Wind Lake in pursuit of panfish, Jim Laganowski and I found ourselves in that in-between time when the bluegills were just about finished with their shoreline spawning activity but hadn't really set up yet in the deep water, where they like to spend the hot summer months.

So we had to look pretty hard to find a few.

Laganowski offered a little encouragement.

"The biggest bluegill I ever saw in my life came out of Wind Lake," he told me. "It measured 11 1/4 inches on a ruler."

This was my first trip to Wind Lake, located in north-central Racine County. Laganowski had fished several times in the past, but mostly through the ice in winter.

"The main target for anglers on Wind Lake is probably panfish," said Doug Welch of the DNR. "They do pretty well on bluegills."

The state stocks 46,800 two- to three-inch walleye fingerlings and 2,300 six- to eight-inch northern pike every other year.

Even so, Welch said, largemouth bass are probably the most popular game fish.

"I'd go early in the morning or evening for bass and try along the shoreline with a surface plug or a Rapala," he said.

The lake also has white bass, yellow bass, rock bass, crappies, perch and sunfish.

When the DNR conducted its last fish survey in 1995, the crew was amazed to find a 47-inch musky.

"We don't stock muskies," Welch said. "They must come in from upstream, from the Fox River system."

Sue Beyler, DNR fisheries biologist for Waukesha County, confirmed Welch's theory.

"It would have to be coming out of Pewaukee Lake to get into the Fox River," Beyler said of the musky. "We don't stock anything else (with muskies) in that system."

Jim Laganowski shows off an eight-inch bluegill caught on Wind Lake in northern Racine County.

The 1995 survey of Wind Lake also showed bass up to 18 inches long and bluegills up to eight inches. The lake also has natural populations of rock bass, white bass, yellow bass, crappies, perch, and sunfish.

Wind Lake is a 936-acre lake with a maximum depth of about 50 feet.

Shallow Means Weeds

"The lake is fairly shallow," Welch said. "It averages about ten feet, so you get a lot of weed growth."

The water is cloudy with algae bloom.

"It's a rich system," Welch explained. "You have nutrients from agricultural runoff."

The DNR operates two free launches, one off Wind Lake Road on the southwest side of the lake, and a new small boat launch on the Wind Lake canal, off Highway 36 on the north side of the lake.

"We're planning to improve the Wind Lake Road launch by putting in a boarding pier within the next three or four years," Welch said.

The Sportsman's Lounge bar and restaurant, at 25313 W. Loomis Road on the north side of the lake, operates a private launch that costs $6, and also has boat rentals. A rowboat costs $15 a day, and a boat and motor go for $30 for four hours, plus $5 for each additional hour.

Laganowski and I launched our boat at the Sportsman's Lounge ramp on a sunny, hot and sweltering afternoon with temperatures in the nineties.

We used ultralight spinning gear with slip bobbers to suspend live bait—a wax worm, a piece of night crawler or a small leech—on either a hook or a small feathered jig.

Tough to Find

At first, we tried to set up out in the middle, but we found so many weeds that it was hard to keep from getting your bait tangled.

So we switched to the shoreline piers and picked up our first bluegill, a nice one that must have been eight or nine inches long. But that was it. We couldn't find any more.

Our luck got a little better when we motored over to Wood Island on the west end of the lake and started to working deep spots in the channel around the island. There, we caught a rock bass and a few nice 'gills, and we caught and released a bunch of smaller ones.

For our last spot, we anchored on the break line near the deepest spot in the lake, where we picked up another bluegill or two, plus one crappie.

So we managed to catch some fish, but we never really figured out a pattern to do it consistently.

"Wind Lake was kind of a tough one," Laganowski said. "I'd like to go back in August or September and try drifting over deep water for the big bluegills."

Maybe next time.

TICHIGAN LAKE/RACINE COUNTY

Miles
0   5

◢ Public boat
   landing

Acreage: **1,132**
Max. depth: **65** feet

FISH PRESENT
- ■ Muskies
- ■ Walleyes
- ■ Northern pike
- ■ Largemouth bass
- ■ Smallmouth bass
- ■ Perch
- ■ Bluegills
- ■ Crappies
- ■ Catfish

**TICHIGAN LAKE
LORE:**

"Panfishing is real
popular on Tichigan
Lake."
— Doug Welch,
DNR

Tichigan Lake

TICHIGAN—When the bobber went down and I set the hook, the unseen fish fought so hard that, at first, I thought it must be a big bass on the line.

As I worked it to the surface of Tichigan Lake, I saw the telltale flash of a short, wide flank looping round and round in tight circles—bluegill style.

"When they spiral like that, they can really put up a fight," Jim Laganowski observed from the other end of the boat.

That bluegill, which measured $8\frac{1}{4}$ inches long, was the first of many we caught on Tichigan Lake, in northwestern Racine County.

"Tichigan is my favorite panfish lake," said Laganowski, who has fished the lake since the 1960s. "It's consistent. I can always come out here and catch a nice mess of bluegills."

Tichigan Lake is a 1,132-acre lake with a maximum depth of 65 feet.

"Part of it's a natural lake and part is a flowage of the Fox River," Laganowski explained.

You can reach the lake from public launches on the Fox River off Bridge Drive, north of the lake, and near the dams in Waterford to the south. In addition, Dooley's Knot Inn, on North Tichigan Road on the northwest side of the lake, operates a private boat landing and offers aluminum rowboat rentals.

Larger Fish than Average

"Panfishing is real popular on Tichigan Lake," said Doug Welch of the DNR. "It's probably above average for productivity. You're going to have more fish and larger fish than the average lake."

Ice fishing is also very productive and popular.

The DNR stocks about 56,000 walleye fingerlings every other year, Welch said.

Jim Laganowski has fished the lake since the 1960s

The lake also has self-sustaining populations of bluegills, crappies, pumpkinseed sunfish, perch, largemouth bass, northern pike, white bass, channel catfish and sheepshead.

"All those species reproduce naturally," Welch said. "There is all kinds of sand and gravel for bass, bluegills, crappies and pumpkinseeds to spawn. There is also an extensive marsh area at the north end of the lake and along the Fox River, which is good spawning habitat for northern pike."

The lake also has coontail weeds and several species of pond weeds.

"That's all good, native aquatic vegetation that provides cover and feeding habitat for fish," Welch said.

In addition, Laganowski said: "There are some smallmouth bass, especially in the river. And an occasional musky makes it through the Pewaukee River into the Fox River to make its home in Tichigan Lake. Muskies over 20 pounds have been caught there. Every year, somebody catches a big one."

We launched Laganowski's jon boat at Dooley's on a September afternoon and motored out in search of feeding bluegills. We found them in weed pockets in about eight feet of water.

That means the fish, which often suspend in deep water during the hot summer months, were already beginning their fall pattern by returning to the shallows as the water cools down.

We used slip-bobber rigs on ultralight spinning gear, with four-pound-test line. The bobbers were set to present the bait—half a night crawler—about four or five feet down.

Different Approaches

I used a small hook with a split-shot about a foot up from the bait, while Laganowski used a small ice jig. It didn't matter. We both caught our share.

"Sometimes I use a wax worm for bluegills or a small tube jig for crappies," Laganowski said.

We fished about four hours, pulling the anchors up and changing the boat's position whenever the action tapered off, but sticking to that eight-foot contour. We picked up three or four bluegills at just about every spot we tried.

We also caught and released a few small bass, plus one large sheepshead that put up a strong fight on that light tackle.

By the time we were done, we had a basket full of more than 20 nice-sized bluegills, plus a perch and a channel cat. The catch provided more than enough fillets for a great fish fry, I'm happy to report.

LAKE MONONA/DANE COUNTY

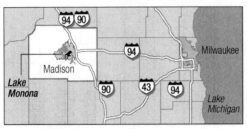

Acreage: **3,274**

Max. depth: **64** feet

FISH PRESENT

■ Muskies
■ Northern pike
■ Walleyes
■ Largemouth bass
■ Smallmouth bass
■ Panfish

LAKE MONONA

"There are some big fish. This June, a local angler caught a 35-pound musky off the Olbrich Park break wall."

— Charlie Grimm, fishing guide

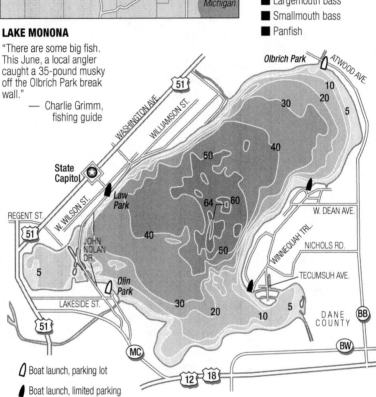

◖ Boat launch, parking lot

◣ Boat launch, limited parking

Lake Monona

MADISON—The silver flash only lasted for an instant, but you could tell it was made by a good-sized fish lunging for the lure.

I was working a white-skirted spinner bait along an inside weed edge on the north side of Lake Monona, when I saw the flash, felt a slam and set the hook.

"Got 'em," I announced to my old friend, Charlie Grimm, who was watching the scene from the other end of the boat. But the way the big bass was power-surging, I really wasn't all that sure.

The fish stayed down with a series of strong, wrist-straining dives that took a while for me to overcome. When I finally did, Grimm was ready with a quick scoop of the net.

"That one had some weight," Grimm said, as I released the fish and we watched it swim off. "We could have used a couple like that in the tournament I fished last weekend."

Grimm, of Madison, is an expert angler with 15 years of experience guiding on the Madison Chain of Lakes. He is active in the Yahara Fishing Club and Four Lakes Bass Masters. Simply put, Grimm knows the Madison lakes better than anyone I know.

Grimm and I fish a Madison-area lake or two together every year. This time, we spent an hour or so catching Lake Monona panfish, sandwiched on either side by a couple of hours of bass-casting Wonder Bread.

At 3,274 acres, Monona is only a third the size of the nearby Lake Mendota, but it has a maximum depth of 64 feet and it offers good fishing for a variety of species. Like the other lakes on the Madison Chain, Monona is an all-around, all-species lake, but each lake has its own special reputation.

"Mendota is the perch lake, Waubesa is the walleye lake and Monona is the bass and bluegill lake," said Kurt Welke, Madison area fisheries manager with the Department of Natural Resources. "And Monona is really coming on strong as a musky lake."

Monona has naturally reproducing populations of largemouth and smallmouth bass, bluegills, perch and crappies. The DNR occasionally

With the Madison skyline as a backdrop, Charlie Grimm unhooks a Lake Monona largemouth bass.

stocks northern pike, walleyes and muskies, and there is some migration of fish from the other lakes on the chain, Welke said.

"I fish Monona about once a week, year-round," said Grimm, who lives just a few blocks from the lake. "There are some big fish. In June, a local angler caught a 35-pound musky off the Olbrich Park break wall."

Madison operates boat launches at Olbrich Park on the east end, Olin Park on the west end and Law Park on the north side; and Monona operates two more launches on the southeast side. The Olbrich and Olin Park launches have large parking lots, but the rest have limited or street parking. There are no boat rentals on the lake.

We launched at Olbrich Park one August evening and, after starting out with a little bass fishing, looked for some panfish.

In past years, I've caught some big bluegills on Monona, either by drifting out in the middle over deep water for suspended fish in the summer or by jigging through the ice on shallow bays in the winter.

This time, we found excellent panfish action with a mixed bag of bluegills and perch hugging tight to the weeds in 12 to 15 feet of water.

On this weekday evening, the lake wasn't crowded at all. There were a few other anglers and water-skiers, but everyone seemed to have plenty of room to spread out and do their thing.

We anchored near an underwater weed hump and used a couple of Grimm's "perch rigs." These are ultralight spinning outfits set up with a heavy slip sinker, followed by a swivel and a 16-inch four-pound-test monofilament leader, tipped with a tiny ice jig dressed with a few spikes.

"The heavy sinker loads the rod and puts a bend in it," Grimm coached. "People who are used to using a little split-shot are put off by the heavy weights. But, with that bend in the rod, you can feel every little nibble."

We just opened the bale and let the bait drop straight down till it hit bottom, then reeled up a crank or two and waited for a bite.

It didn't take long.

In the next hour or so, we caught 15 perch that probably averaged about nine inches long, plus another dozen or so bluegills. We kept the perch for a fish fry, and let most of the bluegills go.

When the panfish bite tapered off, we finished the evening the same way we started out. We motored back to the shallow water, along the inside weed line, and threw more spinner baits till the sun went down.

In addition to the panfish, we ended up catching and releasing a half-dozen largemouth bass, up to about 17 inches long.

That's not bad for a quiet evening on Lake Monona.

LAKE MENDOTA/DANE COUNTY

Acreage: **9,842**
Max. depth: **82** feet

FISH PRESENT
- Walleyes
- Northern pike
- Largemouth bass
- Smallmouth bass
- White bass
- Perch
- Bluegills
- Crappies
- Cisco

LAKE MENDOTA LORE:

"Lake Mendota is best known for perch fishing. But, with special regulations, it has the potential to be one of the best trophy game fish lakes in southern Wisconsin."
— Gary Wroblewski

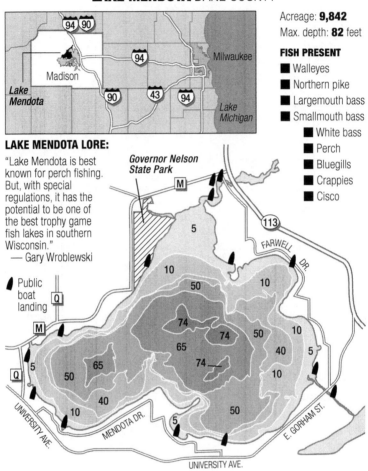

Lake Mendota

MADISON—When the bobber floating off the front end of the boat went under, my son, Rob, set the hook and started reeling.

Before long, we saw the flash of one of those feisty bluegills that use their short, flat bulk to put a major bend in the pole. When Rob hoisted it in, I measured the fish, which was more than nine impressive inches long.

"Congratulations," I announced to Rob and Gary Wroblewski, who was watching a couple of bobbers of his own at the other end of the boat. "You have just broken the family bluegill record."

When the bobber goes down on Madison's Lake Mendota, sometimes you don't really know what you've got on the line.

"The lake offers a tremendous opportunity to fish for a variety of species," said Wroblewski, who has fished the lake for more than 20 years. "It's one of the best multi-species lakes in the region."

Heavily Fished

Mendota is a 9,842-acre lake with a maximum depth of 82 feet. It is both heavily fished and extremely productive.

Perch probably get the most angler attention, both in open water and through the ice.

"We've had years when anglers have taken 650,000 perch, summer and winter combined," said Scot Stewart, fisheries expert with the Department of Natural Resources South Central Region. "In 1988, we estimated Mendota's perch population at more than a million. There's more perch than that right now."

I make a perch trip to Mendota just about every winter. An electronic locater helps you find schools suspended over deep water. But, if you don't have one, just join the crowd. Perch will hit a spike or two hooked on a tiny jig in winter and a spike, wax worm or hellgrammite in the summertime.

In addition to perch, Mendota's variety pack includes northern pike, walleyes, largemouth, smallmouth and white bass, bluegills, crappies and a few muskies.

Gary Wroblewski prepares to release a largemouth bass in Madison's Lake Mendota.

"Lake Mendota is best known for perch fishing," Wroblewski said. "But, with special regulations, it has the potential to be one of the best trophy game fish lakes in southern Wisconsin."

He was referring to special game fish regulations in effect on Lake Mendota which set a 40-inch minimum size limit and a daily bag limit of one for northern pike; an 18-inch size limit and a daily bag limit of three for walleyes; and an 18-inch size limit and a daily bag limit of one for small-mouth and largemouth bass.

"The fishing pressure was too high," Stewart explained. "If we didn't have these higher limits, those fish would be dead."

Instead, Stewart said, anglers are starting to reap the benefits of these special regulations in the form of trophy-size fish.

"For northern pike, we've got one of the prettiest size structures around with lots of fish up to 40 inches and some trickling over," he said.

For walleyes, he said: "The 18-inch limit gives the majority of females a chance to mature and spawn. Occasionally, people take an 11-pounder. It's not going to happen every night, but the potential is there."

Healthy Populations

There are some good-sized largemouth bass, and the smallmouth fishery is tremendous.

"When they're really hitting, you can catch 40 smallmouth bass in a day," Stewart said. "You see them up to 20 inches long, with some longer."

The crappie and bluegill populations are also healthy. "Some of the older bluegills are up to ten inches long," Stewart said.

Mendota also has a sizable white bass population, which you can find by simply trolling a small spoon, spinner or crank bait in open water. I recall one June evening a few years back when my old friend Charlie Grimm and I got into a white bass feeding frenzy, catching and releasing more than we could count.

The lake's forage base includes a cisco population which is recovering from warm-water die-offs in the summers of 1988 and 1989.

The DNR stocks 2,500 northern pike fingerlings and 100,000 walleye fingerlings every other year. Musky stocking was discontinued in 1987 when the DNR opted to concentrate its musky efforts on Monona, Wingra and Waubesa lakes.

There are no fishing boat rentals. But Mazanet Marina, at 55 Bluebill Drive on the north side of the lake, rents pontoon boat for $250 a day, or $150 a half day. "They hold up to ten people," Mike Mazanet said. "If you get ten fishing buddies together, then it's definitely affordable."

Several lakeside parks offer access for shore anglers, and there are lots of public boat launches. The City of Madison has launches at Marshall Park and Spring Harbor on the west side, and Warner and Tenney parks on the east side. Mendota County Park and Governor Nelson State Park also have launches on the north side.

You can catch just about any fish species by suspending a leech or a night crawler under a slip bobber and casting near weeds. That's what Wroblewski, Rob and I did on this June visit. We anchored and worked outside weed edges or weed humps in 9 to 13 feet of water, with the bait anywhere from three to nine feet down.

We caught a few very big bluegills, one nice crappie and a couple largemouth bass using that method. We also saw a beautiful 39-inch northern pike caught and released by another angler in a nearby boat.

As Wroblewski puts it: "Mendota is a great lake to catch all kinds of fish."

LITTLE CEDAR LAKE/WASHINGTON COUNTY

Acreage: **246**
Max. depth: **56** feet

FISH PRESENT
- Northern pike
- Walleyes
- Largemouth bass
- Crappies
- Bluegills
- Sunfish
- Perch

LITTLE CEDAR LAKE LORE:

"It has the potential to produce trophy bass."
— John Nelson, DNR

Little Cedar Lake

WEST BEND—We were casting spinner baits in the weed flat on the north bay of Little Cedar Lake, when I felt a bump and saw the flash of a small, unhooked, hit-and-run northern pike darting away from the bait, almost at boat-side.

A moment later, I looked up to see Don Streeter hoist a similar-sized northern—about 20 inches long—into the boat, before unhooking the fish and watching it swim away.

Those two fish are typical of the northern pike found in Little Cedar Lake, according to John Nelson of the DNR.

A DNR fish survey conducted in the late 1990s found lots of northerns in the 20- to 22-inch range, Nelson said, but only a few at 26 inches, the minimum size for "keepers."

As a result, Nelson said: "My recommendation would be to lower the size limit for northern pike on this lake."

By thinning the northern population a bit, the lake might start to produce some bigger fish, he said. A special regulation to that effect could be implemented in the future.

Little Cedar is a 246-acre lake with a maximum depth of 56 feet located in central Washington County.

"On weekends, it's a busy lake," Nelson said. "But on weekdays, I think you could have a pretty good fishing lake."

In addition to northerns, the lake has self-sustaining populations of largemouth bass, bluegills, crappies, sunfish and perch.

The DNR survey also found lots of bass, including a few up to 18 inches long.

"It has the potential to produce trophy bass," Nelson said.

In addition, since 1999, the DNR has stocked about 24,600 walleye fingerlings every other year in an effort to restore a natural population of walleyes that has dwindled, beginning in the late 1980s. It's too early to say whether the walleye stocking has been successful, Nelson said.

"The Washington County chapter of Walleyes for Tomorrow may do some spawning habitat work, possibly starting in 2006," Nelson said. The

A boat full of anglers casts into the shoreline shade of Little Cedar Lake in central Washington County.

work would involve installing baseball-size rock rubble in parts of the lake or in Cedar Creek, the feeder stream.

Meanwhile panfish—especially bluegills and crappies—get the most attention from anglers, Nelson believes.

Little Cedar has one public boat landing in Ackerman's Grove Park, off Highway Z on the southeast side of the lake. It costs $5 to launch a boat. There is also a fishing pier near the launch for shore anglers.

Knight's Boat Rental, 3986 Highway NN and Z, on the north side of the lake, rents fishing boats. A rowboat costs $9, plus $3 for each additional angler.

I fished Little Cedar Lake on two June afternoons with Don Streeter and Chuck Smrcina.

Little Cedar has many of the elements of a good bass lake—lily pads, submerged weeds, some steep drop-offs and overhanging trees. We worked all of those areas, plus the piers, with medium-action spinning gear and plastic worms and frogs or Rapala minnow lures, but only managed to find a few small bass in the 12-inch range.

We were hoping to locate some bigger bass by switching to spinners on the weed flats, but instead, we encountered those northerns, plus a couple more.

"The bass could be done with the spawn and in that period when they're resting," said Streeter, a guide and bass tournament angler. "This may be a better summer lake than a spring lake. I'd come back when the bass are set up in their summer pattern and not so scattered. I'd try fishing the slop on the south end, and maybe work the outside weed line at the deep holes with plastics and crank baits."

Meanwhile, we decided to try for some panfish.

We anchored among scattered weed pockets in about five feet of water, set up slip-bobber rigs and started soaking live bait for panfish. We suspended pieces of night crawler about two feet down on a small hook or jig.

It didn't take long for the bobbers to go down.

For the next hour, we had steady action catching a dozen or so bluegills and crappies. Some of them were as big as your hand.

Trout

J. Riepenhoff

Trout

J. Ripenhof

Each spring, just for the fun of it, the Department of Natural Resources stocks several southern Wisconsin lakes with legal-size trout for put-and-take trout fishing.

These lakes are stocked with hatchery trout, mostly browns and rainbows, which provide some great early season trout fishing opportunities. The trout are all about 9 to 12 inches long when stocked. They are not expected to reproduce. Although most are caught and kept during the first weeks of the fishing season, the lakes are deep enough and have cold enough water so that a few trout survive from year to year. Every once in a while you hear of someone catching a big one, 20 inches or longer.

The trout are relatively easy to catch and are generally active in the cool, early spring water, before fishing for other species heats up. The hardest part is locating the trout, since they move around and don't seem to relate to any specific structure. I like to keep my boat moving, either drifting or using the electric trolling motor, until I get that first bite. Then it's time to anchor, because the trout tend to cluster in schools.

I've hooked many of these trout on a small minnow suspended beneath a slip bobber. Some anglers prefer to cast a fly, which works on days when it's not too windy. My favorite method is casting spinners because the trout really hit them hard and sometimes become airborne.

Two of my favorite trout lakes—Lower Nashotah and Horseshore—are profiled in this chapter. In addition, Lower Genesee, Fowler and Beulah lakes, which are included in other chapters, are also stocked with trout each year. Other trout lakes worth a try include Ottawa, in Waukesha County, and Waubesee, in Racine County. Moose Lake, in Waukesha County, may also start getting stocked with trout in the future.

Because of budget cuts, the DNR has suspended trout stocking in 2004 and 2005. Trout stocking may resume after that.

NEMAHBINS/NASHOTAH LAKES/WAUKESHA COUNTY

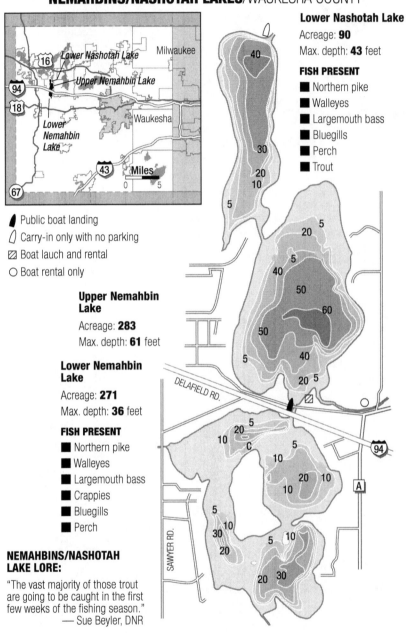

Lower Nashotah Lake

Acreage: **90**

Max. depth: **43** feet

FISH PRESENT

- ■ Northern pike
- ■ Walleyes
- ■ Largemouth bass
- ■ Bluegills
- ■ Perch
- ■ Trout

(inset map labels:) Lower Nashotah Lake · Milwaukee · Upper Nemahbin Lake · Waukesha · Lower Nemahbin Lake · Miles · 0 · 5 · 16 · 94 · 18 · 43 · 67

🡒 Public boat landing

◖ Carry-in only with no parking

▨ Boat lauch and rental

○ Boat rental only

Upper Nemahbin Lake

Acreage: **283**

Max. depth: **61** feet

Lower Nemahbin Lake

Acreage: **271**

Max. depth: **36** feet

FISH PRESENT

- ■ Northern pike
- ■ Walleyes
- ■ Largemouth bass
- ■ Crappies
- ■ Bluegills
- ■ Perch

NEMAHBINS/NASHOTAH LAKE LORE:

"The vast majority of those trout are going to be caught in the first few weeks of the fishing season."
— Sue Beyler, DNR

Lower Nashotah, Upper Nemahbin and Lower Nemahbin Lakes

DELAFIELD—We hadn't been anchored long, watching the bobbers bob in the choppy water of Lower Nashotah lake, when one of them went under.

"There's one!" Jim Laganowski shouted, as he set the hook, reeled, then grabbed the landing net to scoop up our first trout of the day.

Though we both had fished the adjacent Upper and Lower Nemahbin lakes in past years, neither of us had ever ventured through the channel that leads to Lower Nashotah Lake to fish for trout.

It was definitely worth the trip.

What we caught that cloudy day in May were hatchery trout, according to Sue Beyler of the DNR. The DNR stocks seven thousand "catchable size" trout in Lower Nashotah each year, three thousand rainbows and four thousand browns, Beyler said.

"It's basically just to provide another recreational fishing opportunity on a lake," she said.

Although Lower Nashotah—at 90 acres with a maximum depth of 43 feet—is deep enough that some of the trout carry over from year to year, Beyler said: "The vast majority of those trout are going to be caught in the first few weeks of the fishing season."

The DNR also maintains put-and-take trout fishing on Lower Genesee, Ottawa and Fowler lakes in Waukesha County. "It provides an early season fishing opportunity before the water warms up and the bass become active," Beyler said.

Getting to Lower Nashotah takes a small boat and a little effort. Except for a carry-in access on the north end of the lake, there is no boat launch on Lower Nashotah, so the only way to get there is to cross Upper Nemahbin.

That's what we did.

185

Jim Laganowski unhooks a trout caught on Lower Nashotah Lake, which is accessible through a small channel from Upper Nemahbin Lake.

Laganowski's 14-foot jon boat was perfect for the job. We launched it at the public boat landing on Delafield Road, hunched down as we slowly motored beneath the low highway overpass and set out across Upper Nemahbin in search of the channel to Lower Nashotah.

Rental Boats Available

If you don't have a small boat, the Channel Inn, at 34422 Delafield Road across the street from the public launch, rents them; as does Al's Bait, further east on Delafield Road. The Channel Inn also operates a boat launch.

The channel to Lower Nashotah is narrow and easy to miss. It's also very shallow. Even in a flat-bottom jon boat, we had to use the oars to push-pole our way through spots where the water was less than a foot deep.

Once we got to the lake, we anchored off a point in about 12 feet of water. We used ultralight slip-bobber rigs to suspend small fathead minnows three to five feet down. That method produced a couple "keeper" trout, plus some "throw backs" that didn't quite reach the nine-inch minimum length.

Our bobber fishing also produced some surprise catch-and-release action with a few largemouth and smallmouth bass, all in the 12- to 13-inch range.

But the best trout action of the day came after we lifted the anchor and moved to another spot where we saw some trout rising. This time, we started throwing and trolling small spinners and, before long, we each had our three-trout limit. It was a mixed bag of browns and rainbows that ranged from just over 9 to 11$\frac{1}{2}$ inches long.

Popular Destination

The adjacent Nemahbin lakes are also popular among anglers, as anyone who travels I-94 between Milwaukee and Madison can attest.

"The main species out there would probably be largemouth bass and bluegills," Beyler said. "Walleyes would be secondary, along with smallmouths and northern pike."

The two lakes have 554 acres, combined. Upper Nemahbin's maximum depth is 61 feet, while Lower Nemahbin's is 36 feet.

Both lakes have good weeds and structure, including drop-offs and points on Upper Nemahbin and deep holes and basins with shallow areas in between on Lower Nemahbin.

"The Nemahbins are stocked as a single unit," Beyler said. "We stock right at the boat launch between the two lakes so they can go either way."

Stocking quotas call for 55,500 two-inch walleye fingerlings and 6,244 four- to six-inch northern pike fingerlings every other year. The bass and panfish populations, including rock bass, are self-sustaining.

Every now and then, you hear reports of somebody catching a big northern pike on Lower Nashotah or one of the Nemahbins.

"That may be," Beyler said. "Trout would make really good northern pike food."

HORSESHOE LAKE/MANITOWOC COUNTY

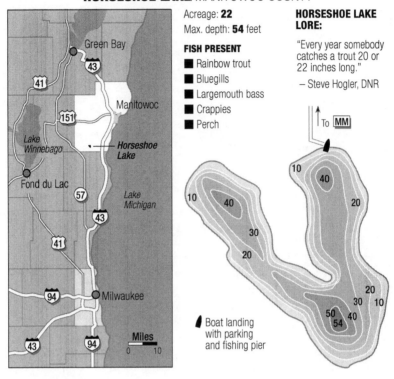

Acreage: **22**
Max. depth: **54** feet

FISH PRESENT
- Rainbow trout
- Bluegills
- Largemouth bass
- Crappies
- Perch

HORSESHOE LAKE LORE:

"Every year somebody catches a trout 20 or 22 inches long."

– Steve Hogler, DNR

Boat landing with parking and fishing pier

Horseshoe Lake

S PRING VALLEY—Peace and quiet, plenty of tree-lined shore and a chance to hook into a beautiful rainbow trout.

If you find that combination appealing, consider paying a visit to Horseshoe Lake.

That's what Jim Laganowski and I did one recent morning.

Laganowski had fished Horseshoe Lake before, but this was my first trip to this pretty little gem of a lake in southern Manitowoc County.

The first thing I noticed about this lake was the absence of any noise from outboards or jet skies. A special regulation prohibits the use of outboard motors.

For me, that's a good thing.

At just 22 acres, Horseshoe Lake is small enough to paddle, or use an electric trolling motor, to fish all the way around in just a few hours.

"For somebody who likes to fish out of a canoe or a small car-top boat, this lake is perfect," Laganowski said.

There is a free boat landing and a pier for shore anglers located off Highway XX on the north side of the lake. There are no boat rentals.

According to Steve Hogler, fisheries biologist with the Department of Natural Resources at Mishicot, the state stocks about 2,200 rainbow trout fingerlings, about six to eight inches long, each fall.

"The trout stocking is essentially put-and-take, although there are some holdovers," Hogler said. "The water is good quality, spring-fed and cold. A few fish survive to the next year. Every year somebody catches a trout 20 or 22 inches long."

The daily bag limit for trout is five, with a minimum length of seven inches. A special extended trout season runs from the first Saturday in May through March 1.

"People fish trout through the ice," Hogler said.

In addition to the stocked trout, Horseshoe Lake has naturally reproducing populations of largemouth bass and bluegills, plus a few crappies and perch.

"Most people fish the trout or the bluegills," Hogler said.

A rainbow trout from 22-acre Horseshoe Lake in southern Manitowoc County.

When we launched my jon boat at the public landing on an overcast spring morning with occasional drizzle, Laganowski and I had trout on our minds.

The crystal clear water and the steep drop-off, just a few feet from shore, looked promising. This lake is small, but it's 54 feet down at its deepest point.

There's a cluster of homes and cabins, but much of the shoreline, including the peninsula that bisects the "horseshoe," remains natural and undeveloped.

At first, we used ultralight spinning gear with two- or four-pound monofilament to throw little spinners at the weeds, submerged logs and other shoreline structure, as we slowly made our way around the lake.

The first few fish we caught and released were largemouth bass.

It wasn't until we left the shoreline and moved out to deeper water that we connected with our first rainbow trout.

"The fish were deep," Laganowski said afterward. "But they came up and hit those spinners."

So we made several drifts, casting over the deep water.

Before long, we had four nice rainbows in the boat, all in the 10- to 12-inch range.

Some of our fish jumped, affording quick glimpses of their silver sides with iridescent red flanks. We lost a feisty rainbow that shook off during one such maneuver.

Suddenly, the wind shifted, a light rain started falling and the fish shut down. We had a few more bumps from light-hitting trout that didn't hook up, and then nothing at all.

But we hung in there, drifting and casting in the rain for another hour or longer, and finally our persistence paid off.

I made one more cast and felt a big fish come up from the depths and hit the spinner hard. This one didn't jump, opting instead to make a series of power surges and dives.

Things were out of control for close to five minutes before Laganowski managed a quick scoop that got the big rainbow in the net.

At 15 inches long with a wide girth, this was probably one of those "holdover" trout that survive into a second fishing season.

One thing's for sure. It was the fish of the day.

Northern Pike

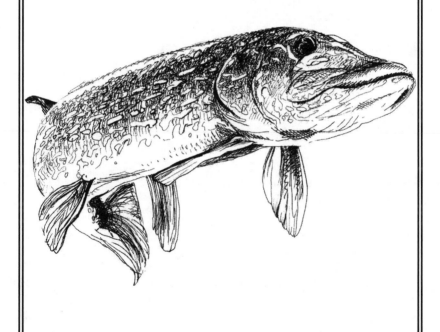

Northern Pike

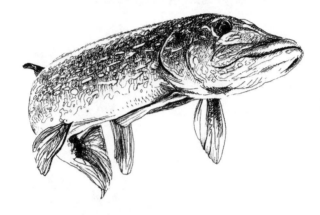

JRiepenhofX

S pear-headed, sharp-toothed and feisty, the northern pike is a powerful predator exceeded in size only by the mighty muskellunge.
Known as aggressive feeders, northern pike are sometimes called
"water wolves." Experienced anglers know when they have one on long
before they see the fish because a northern, when hooked, launches into an
unmistakable power surge that is pure muscle.

Northerns are found in many southern Wisconsin lakes. In 1995,
because of concerns about declining northern pike populations attributed
to increased fishing pressure and a loss of spawning habitat, the state established a 31-county northern pike restoration zone in southern and central
Wisconsin, where the daily bag limit on most lakes was changed from five
northerns with no size limit to two northerns with a 26-inch size limit.

Fishing pressure on northerns remains heavy, both in open water and
through the ice. It's too early to tell whether the new regulations are working. But early indications are that northern pike populations are improving
on some lakes because the regulations allow the fish to reach spawning age.

Still, trophy pike are few and far between because so many fish are caught and kept when they reach the legal length of 26 inches.

Mendota, Geneva and Delavan lakes have special trophy northern pike regulations designed to produce bigger fish. On Mendota, the daily bag limit is one pike, 40 inches or longer; and on Geneva and Delavan, the daily bag limit is one pike, 32 inches or longer. I wouldn't be surprised to see trophy pike regulations on more lakes in the future.

By the time the general fishing season opens in May, northern pike have already finished spawning, and can be found in weed pockets, weed edges or rocky areas adjacent to weeds in about six to ten feet of water. Cast a small bucktail or bass spinner and hang on tight for some explosive action.

When summer arrives, the shallow weeds still hold some northerns, but the big pike move to 25 or 30 feet of water. Look for them near the thermocline, where the warm surface water meets the cool water. A one-ounce jig tipped with a plastic lure or a piece of frozen smelt, or a Lindy-rigged creek chub on a circle hook can both be productive, as can trolling big crank baits.

In fall, the pike move back to the weed edges. Try soaking a big golden shiner or a small musky sucker on a slip-bobber rig near the outside edge of green weeds.

Pike remain active in cold water and many are taken by ice anglers who set tip-ups baited with a shiner or piece of frozen smelt, or twitch jigging spoons with short jigging rods. A steel leader on your tip-up line will prevent most bite-offs.

My personal best is a 40-inch northern that I caught in Canada years ago. But I hooked one at least that big while crank bait fishing for smallmouth bass on Lake Mendota a few years back. We didn't have a net, so I lost that one at the boat. But it was great to tangle with a trophy-size pike on a southern Wisconsin lake.

Big Muskego and Geneva lakes are profiled in this chapter. Northerns can also be caught on Okauchee, Oconomowoc, Pewaukee, Moose, Big Green, Big Cedar and Mendota lakes, which are included in other chapters. For action, try Big Muskego. For a trophy, try Geneva, Big Green, Big Cedar or Mendota.

GENEVA LAKE/WALWORTH COUNTY

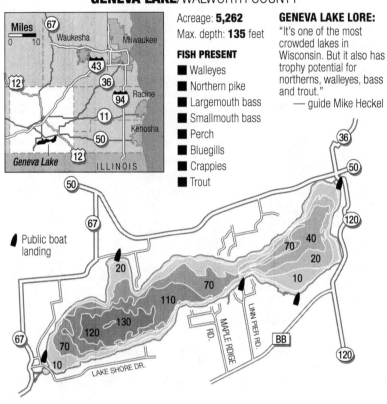

Acreage: **5,262**
Max. depth: **135** feet

FISH PRESENT

- Walleyes
- Northern pike
- Largemouth bass
- Smallmouth bass
- Perch
- Bluegills
- Crappies
- Trout

GENEVA LAKE LORE:
"It's one of the most crowded lakes in Wisconsin. But it also has trophy potential for northerns, walleyes, bass and trout."

— guide Mike Heckel

Public boat landing

Geneva Lake

WILLIAMS BAY—With utmost care, I gently dropped a big, lip-hooked live creek chub over the side of the boat and let a Lindy-rigged egg sinker take it all the way down to the bottom of Geneva Lake.

In this case, the bottom was more than 30 feet straight down, where the warm water meets the cold and many a toothy northern pike likes to linger on a hot summer day.

"Leave the bale open," guide Mike Heckel coached. "When you feel a bite, give 'em a little line. But don't wait too long and don't set the hook. Just start reeling."

When I felt a quick jab, I did exactly as I was told and, soon, felt the rod-bending weight, stubborn resistance and awesome power surges of my first Geneva Lake northern.

It turned out to be one of many that we caught that day.

For years, I had avoided Lake Geneva because of its reputation for being crowded with water skiers, sailers and other pleasure boaters. I didn't realize that I was missing out on some first-class fishing opportunities.

"It's one of the most crowded lakes in Wisconsin," said Heckel, who is past president of the Lake Geneva Fishing Club and has guided on the lake for 26 years. "But it also has trophy potential for northerns, walleyes, bass and trout."

Don't Be Late

In fact, the state record inland brown trout—which weighed 18 pounds 6 ounces—was caught in Geneva Lake by Terry McKittrick back in 1984.

Geneva is a deep, clear 5,262-acre lake with a maximum depth of 135 feet.

"It's a tremendous fishing lake," said Rick Dauffenbach, fisheries technician with the DNR at Sturtevant. "It's such a big, deep lake that there is plenty of space for those fish."

199

Guide Mike Heckel shows off a healthy northern pike he caught at Geneva Lake in Walworth County.

Because of the crowding, it's a good idea to fish Geneva Lake at night or in the early morning hours. If you go in the morning, plan on launching by about 5:30 A.M. to ensure a parking spot, and quitting by about 10 A.M. when the boat traffic gets intense.

"I fish midnight to 6 A.M. for walleyes or bass in July and August," said Heckel, of Waterford. "The fish get driven into nocturnal patterns by the boats and jet skiers. You can still catch fish early in the morning, but your odds go up at night."

Zingle's Boat Line in Lake Geneva and Geneva Lake Bait and Tackle on Highway 67, south of Highway 50 in the Township of Delavan, rent fishing boats. At Geneva Lake, you have to make an appointment the day before you rent. There are public boat landings in Williams Bay on the northwest side of the lake; Fontana on the west end; Linn Pier Road and Hillside Road on the south; and in downtown Lake Geneva on the east end.

Geneva Lake has self-sustaining populations of largemouth and small-mouth bass, northern pike, panfish, white bass and ciscoes, plus a forage population of mimic shiners. In addition, the DNR stocks lake trout and brown trout every year and walleyes every other year. The 2001 stocking quota was 3,000 brown trout, 20,000 lake trout and 263,000 walleye fingerlings.

Strict Regulations

A special regulation sets a minimum length of 32 inches for northern pike with a daily bag limit of one. "That was to create a trophy northern fishery," Dauffenbach said. "It was thought that Lake Geneva had the potential to produce trophy northern pike if we just gave them a chance to grow."

A survey in spring of 2000 showed the average female northern pike was 23 inches long, up from 20.5 inches in 1995 when the special regulation began; and the average male northern was 18.6 inches, up from 17.7.

Heckel called the lake "species specific." "That means, at certain times of the year, one species of fish will be the easiest to catch," he said.

Dauffenbach agreed. "May is the smallmouth month," he said. "In June it's the largemouths, July can be a crap shoot, in August and September there is tremendous northern pike fishing, lake trout fishing is good in September, and the crappies are active in September and October."

Trout anglers troll in 90 to 120 feet of water with Lake Michigan-type down-riggers, Heckel said. And in winter, he said, there is good ice fishing for northerns and panfish in "The Flats" area, off the Hillside Road launch.

For our trip, I met Heckel at the Williams Bay launch early one foggy July morning. Even though the prime time for smallmouths was over, we tried to locate some.

"When the smallmouths turn on, 15- to 30-fish days are not uncommon." Heckel said. "But in summer, it's hit or miss."

We used four-pound-test monofilament, a hook and split-shot to drag half night crawlers along the bottom as we drifted the break line in 18 to 21 feet of water. We caught a few nice bluegills, perch and rock bass, but the smallies eluded us.

So we shifted gears to pursue northerns and had some great action. This time, we hooked a sucker or creek chub on Lindy rigs with half-ounce egg sinkers tied to 12-pound-test monofilament without any leader.

"If you use a leader, you won't get half the bites," Heckel said.

We also used special "circle hooks," designed to prevent deep-hooking fish and expedite catch and release.

"The hook curls around almost into a circle," Heckel explained. "When the northern hits the chub, he swallows it. You don't set the hook, you just reel and apply pressure and you end up hooking the northern in the corner of his mouth."

We worked rock piles, humps and deep weed lines near the thermocline in about 32 to 36 feet of water with deeper water around the structure. For the next couple of hours, we had fast action, catching and releasing a dozen strong, beautifully colored northerns, up to 33 inches long.

BIG MUSKEGO LAKE/WAUKESHA COUNTY

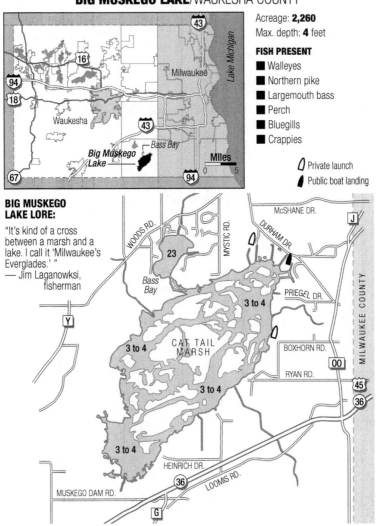

Acreage: **2,260**
Max. depth: **4** feet

FISH PRESENT
- Walleyes
- Northern pike
- Largemouth bass
- Perch
- Bluegills
- Crappies

◖ Private launch
◣ Public boat landing

BIG MUSKEGO LAKE LORE:

"It's kind of a cross between a marsh and a lake. I call it 'Milwaukee's Everglades.' "
— Jim Laganowksi, fisherman

Big Muskego Lake

MUSKEGO—My first cast had barely hit the water when an unseen force swirled up and slammed the spinner bait with the kind of fierce power-surge that can only be delivered by a northern pike.

"The guys at work call this place 'Little Canada,'" Jim Laganowski told me as I unhooked the fish and watched it swim away. "Where else can you get this kind of northern action around here?"

That's a good question.

It may come as a surprise to learn that our northern pike hot spot is Big Muskego Lake, which, not long ago, was a polluted, carp-infested swamp with a reputation as a local "Dead Sea."

Fortunately, all that has changed, thanks to a major habitat rehabilitation, carp eradication and game fish stocking project begun in 1995.

Today, Big Muskego Lake, located in the southeast corner of Waukesha County, has emerged as a born-again fishery with panfish, largemouth bass, walleyes and plenty of feisty northern pike.

"We went from a carp-infested swamp to northern pike heaven," said Sue Beyler of the DNR.

Big Muskego is a shallow, 2,260-acre lake with an average depth of just three feet.

"It's really a big cattail marsh," Beyler said.

Laganowski, a skilled fisherman who frequents Big Muskego Lake, calls it "Milwaukee's Everglades."

Anglers were starting to reap the benefits of the restored fishery when disaster struck in the form of a winter kill in January of 2001.

Fish can suffer winter kill when lake water, beneath the ice, lacks the green weeds and sunlight needed to produce sufficient oxygen. That winter, heavy snowfall on the ice and rotting cattails underneath made for a deadly combination.

"I would say that 75 percent of the fish in the main lake probably died," said Beyler. Most of the fish that died were bass and bluegills, she said.

"Northern pike and perch are somewhat more tolerant of low oxygen, and most of them were probably able to get to better water, " she said.

Jim Laganowski hoists up another feisty northern pike from the restored fishery at Big Muskego Lake.

A channel on the northwest side of the lake leads to the 100-acre Bass Bay, which has deep water, down to 23 feet. The DNR installed aerators there in the winter of 2001 to ensure adequate oxygen levels. The inlet from Little Muskego Lake, south of the Bass Channel, also provided some fresh, oxygen-rich water that saved more fish.

"Bass Bay didn't winter kill at all," Beyler said. "Bass Bay and the inlet were our reservoirs of live fish, so that some fish would stay alive and repopulate the lake."

In addition to the northerns and perch, she said: "We had quite a few bass and bluegills that made it by migrating to those areas."

When Laganowski, of Franklin, and I visited the Big Muskego one July day, we launched his jon boat at the Boxhorn's Gun Club ramp, off Boxhorn Road on the lake's east side. Hunter's Nest gun club has another private launch off Schultz Road on the north. The City of Muskego operates a public launch off Durham Road on the north, but there are no boat rentals on the lake.

The bays and channels that wind through tall cattails provide a sense of wilderness solitude just minutes from downtown Milwaukee. But they can also make it easy for a newcomer to get lost. Laganowski recommends bringing a compass along, and paying attention to landmarks.

According to Beyler, the habitat project included a year-and-a-half-long water drawdown to let the lake bottom compact and kill undesirable aquatic plants; construction of three nest islands by Ducks Unlimited to enhance waterfowl production and improve hunting; netting and transfer to other lakes of remaining game fish and panfish; poisoning of the remaining fish, mostly carp; installation of a carp barrier at the lake's outlet near Muskego Dam Road; and restocking the lake with native fish.

"We figure we probably killed 350,000 pounds of carp," Beyler said.

The lake was then refilled and the DNR began stocking millions of fish, including: 2.4 million northern pike fry and 56,000 northern fingerlings; 1.7 million walleye fry; 21,000 largemouth bass fingerlings, plus 500 adult bass eight to twelve inches long; 70,000 yellow perch fingerlings and 25,000 adult perch five to nine inches long; 200,000 bluegills four to eight inches long; 800 black crappies and 200 white crappies five to seven inches long.

"Altogether, by the end of summer 1998, we stocked a total of 5.4 million fish in Big Muskego Lake and Bass Bay," Beyler said.

Fishing reopened in spring of 1997 with special regulations that remain in place to protect the restored fishery. Anglers can keep just one bass a day, 18 inches or longer; and a total of 15 panfish, eight inches or longer. The

15-inch, five-fish daily bag limit for walleyes, and the 26-inch, two-fish bag limit for northerns are similar to other southern Wisconsin lakes.

With the special regulations, Big Muskego's fishing is coming back strong.

"By summer of 1998, people were starting to catch legal size panfish," Beyler said. "And there are plenty of northerns over 26 inches."

The DNR plans to stock 10,000 four- to six-inch northern pike fingerlings a year to replenish those taken by anglers, both from open water and through the ice in winter, Beyler said, while the other species don't appear to require more stocking.

After the winter kill to further restore the fishery, in spring of 2001 the DNR stocked 2.1 million quarter-inch northern pike fry and 20,000 one-inch northern pike fingerlings; 70,000 one- to two-inch largemouth bass fingerlings; and 46,900 panfish—bluegills, sunfish, crappies, and perch. Those fish were in addition to the lake's regular quota of northerns that were stocked in 2001 and 2002.

Laganowski and I fished a few different spots, anchoring at some and drifting through others, by casting spinners or top-water baits. Since the water is shallow, the fish relate to cattail edges or submerged weeds.

We worked our baits along the edges and caught a bunch of northerns, plus a few bass and panfish. None of our northerns reached the 26-inch limit for keepers, but a few came very close.

"What these fish lack in size, they make up in numbers," Laganowski said. "Right now, I don't think there's a more productive lake in this part of the state."

And the fish will only get bigger.

Muskies

J. Ruyenhoft

Muskies

J. Rupenhoft

Elusive, unpredictable, fierce and just plain big, the muskellunge has seized a lock-jaw hold on our collective imagination like no other fish. Witness the icon-like status claimed by countless taxidermy mounts that hang prominently in taverns and sporting goods stores across the state, causing people to stop, stare and dream.

There is a saying about the musky's place at the top of the freshwater food chain that goes: "all other fish are just bait."

Sometimes called "the fish of ten thousand casts," the musky is next to impossible to predict. Some fish for years and never hook one. Not even the most skilled professional can catch them every day. Despite the difficulty of catching a musky, or maybe because of it, no other fish is more highly prized by anglers.

A musky will follow a lure to the boat without fear, attack it the instant it hits the water, or simply ignore it altogether. Musky anglers talk enthusiastically about "follows," the muskies they saw that never struck the lure.

Although the legal limit for a "keeper" musky is 34 inches on most lakes, that number has become all but irrelevant in recent years, as voluntary catch-and-release has become the standard operating procedure among most musky anglers. Muskies are rarely killed for food. Some anglers release all muskies, while others keep only a trophy fish for a taxidermy mount. When the time comes, that decision is strictly a personal one. Like beauty itself, what constitutes a trophy musky is something that exists only in the eye of the beholder and is probably linked to a personal best.

Those of us afflicted with "musky fever" can't help but dream of some day surpassing the world record fish, a 69-pound, 11-ounce monster caught by Louie Spray on the Chippewa Flowage in northern Wisconsin on October 20, 1949.

Although the musky is native to northern waters, stocking has produced some excellent musky lakes in southern Wisconsin. A little know-how and a lot of persistence will catch these fish.

In spring, when muskies are starting to feed after the rigors of spawning, it's best to use small lures, four to six inches long. Cast a bucktail spinner, twitch bait, jerk bait or crank bait along outside weed edges and weed pockets adjacent to musky spawning areas, shallow marshy areas or weed flats.

In summer when the surface water reaches about 65 degrees, start using top-waters and bigger lures, up to about ten inches long, and speed up your retrieve.

On lakes where it is permitted, trolling can be very productive in mid- to late summer and into the fall. As the surface water warms up, some muskies find more comfortable temperatures by suspending in deep water at the thermocline, where the warm surface water meets the cool, deep water. The bait fish that muskies feed on do the same thing. Trolling different sized crank baits on a long line, a downrigger, or a planer board—or a combination of those methods—can be deadly. I've had a few five-musky trolling days.

Trolling the west basin of Pewaukee Lake, keeping the lures in the 15- to 20-foot contour, is relatively easy. On Okauchee and Oconomowoc lakes, the contour is irregular and hard to follow, so you're better off trolling deep water and looking for schools of bait fish on your locater.

In fall, trolling is still an option, but many anglers return to casting the weed lines. Use bigger lures, up to ten inches or longer, and add a live sucker, suspended beneath a bobber on a quick-strike rig, to the mix. A quick-strike rig allows you to release the musky unharmed. Start with a 12-inch sucker in early fall and increase the size up to 18 inches by late November. When muskies are bulking up for the winter, an 18-inch bait fish isn't too big.

Pewaukee, Okauchee, Oconomowoc, Fowler and Wingra lakes are profiled in this chapter. LaBelle, Little Green and Monona lakes, which are included in other chapters, also offer good musky fishing. I'd try Pewaukee or Wingra to catch numbers of fish, and Okauchee for a trophy, although Pewaukee also produces some big ones every year.

I caught my biggest musky on a jerk bait cast along an Oconomowoc Lake drop-off on a cloudy June morning in 2001. It was 48 inches long and weighed 28 pounds.

PEWAUKEE LAKE/WAUKESHA COUNTY

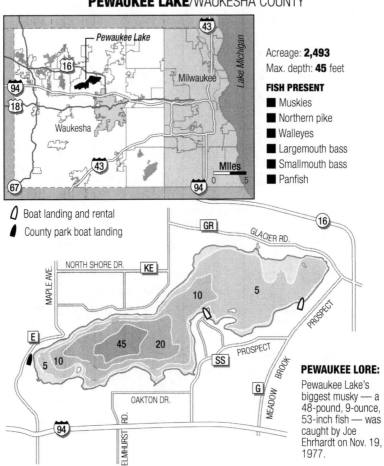

Acreage: **2,493**
Max. depth: **45** feet

FISH PRESENT
- Muskies
- Northern pike
- Walleyes
- Largemouth bass
- Smallmouth bass
- Panfish

Miles
0   5

◖ Boat landing and rental
◗ County park boat landing

PEWAUKEE LORE:

Pewaukee Lake's biggest musky — a 48-pound, 9-ounce, 53-inch fish — was caught by Joe Ehrhardt on Nov. 19, 1977.

Pewaukee Lake

PEWAUKEE—One of the hardest-fished and most consistently productive lakes in Wisconsin is located less than a half-hour drive from downtown Milwaukee.

We're talking, of course, about Pewaukee Lake.

Even among anglers, Pewaukee Lake means different things to different people.

Some like to anchor off Rocky Point to fish for walleyes.

Others prefer to cast the scattered weed pockets for largemouth bass or the rocky humps for smallmouths.

Still others may opt to rent a boat to bobber fish for panfish or cast from shore or the fishing pier at Pewaukee Village's Lake Park on the east end of the lake.

Come winter, a lot of people like to jig through the ice for panfish or set tip-ups for northerns and walleyes.

And, in recent years, Pewaukee Lake has emerged as a musky angler's Mecca.

"Pewaukee Lake is one of the finest lakes in this state in terms of number and size of muskies," said Ron Groeschl, vice president of the Milwaukee Chapter of the Muskies Inc. fishing organization.

An article in the June 2000 issue of Muskie, the official publication of Muskies Inc., ranks Pewaukee Lake sixth in the United States for the number of muskies 50 inches or longer caught and released by club members.

In 1995, according to Muskies Inc. records, the lake produced a remarkable nine muskies 50 inches or longer.

Sue Beyler of the DNR calls Pewaukee Lake "a very good all-around, all-species fishing lake" with healthy, naturally reproducing populations of bass and panfish.

Back in the 1980s, most Pewaukee Lake anglers were after largemouth bass. But in recent years, the muskellunge has surpassed the bass as the angler's fish of choice, Beyler said.

A Department of Natural Resources study found that, in 1998, 47 percent of the angler effort on the lake was directed at muskies and that musky fishing pressure had nearly tripled from 1982 to 1998.

Silhouetted against a sunset and the water of Pewaukee Lake, guide Steve Miljat casts for muskies.

According to Beyler, the state stocking program calls for five thousand musky fingerlings each year and 249,300 walleye fingerlings every other year.

In addition, each year since 1986, Muskies Inc. has stocked about 200 to 400 12- to 18-inch muskies from the club's rearing pond in Delafield.

Pewaukee Lake muskies have above average growth rates compared to other Class A musky lakes in the state.

"The average length for a harvested musky increased from 30 inches in 1982 to 44 inches in 1998," Beyler said.

Yet, thanks to efforts by Muskies Inc. to promote catch and release, very few anglers are keeping muskies these days. In 1998, only 48 of the estimated 2,782 muskies caught by anglers were kept.

Northern pike stocking, which had been set at five thousand fingerlings a year, was discontinued as of 2001 because of "competition for food and possible predation on muskies," Beyler said.

Even so, northern pike fishing, which is particularly popular among ice anglers, is expected to continue with a self-sustaining, naturally reproducing population.

"The Pewaukee Lake Sanitary District is acquiring land along the southeast and north sides of the lake which they plan to restore as marshland for northern pike spawning habitat," Beyler said.

The 2,493-acre lake has public boat launches on Lakeview Boulevard, off Highway SS on the south side of the lake; off Highway E on the west side; and near Smokey's Bait Shop, at 129 Park Avenue, on the east side.

Boat and motor rentals are available at both Smokey's Bait Shop and Smokey's Muskellunge Shop, at N27-W2745 Woodland Drive, near the Lakeview Boulevard launch.

In addition to Lake Park, there is also public access for shore fishing near the launch on the west end.

Because it is so close to Milwaukee and such a good lake to fish, I visit Pewaukee Lake about a half-dozen times a year, which is probably more than any other lake. I've caught some nice bass and some very big walleyes over the years. But, like others, most of my time on the lake is spent in pursuit of muskies.

I learned much of what I know about Pewaukee Lake from Steve Miljat, who spends a good part of his life guiding and fishing the lake.

In 1995, Miljat caught two huge Pewaukee Lake muskies, a 50$\frac{1}{2}$-incher and a 52$\frac{1}{2}$-incher, which was the largest released musky in the state that year.

In ten years of fishing with Steve, we have boated some nice muskies and even had a few four- and five-musky days.

"What makes Pewaukee Lake unique is that it's two lakes in one," Miljat said. "The western basin is deep and the eastern basin is shallow, so the water in the east warms up a lot faster than in the west."

From opening day till about the Fourth of July, our strategy is to cast the weed lines and weed flats. In the heat of summer, from July till mid-September, we switch to trolling the deep water of the western basin where the muskies seek cool water temperatures and bait fish. In fall, we cast and troll. And, in November, we add some sucker fishing to that mix.

One thing that keeps Miljat going is his belief that Pewaukee Lake has the potential to produce a 50-pound musky.

"With the numerous 30-pound fish that have been caught in recent years and the growing popularity of the catch-and-release ethic, I think there's a good chance that it will happen," he said.

OKAUCHEE LAKE/WAUKESHA COUNTY

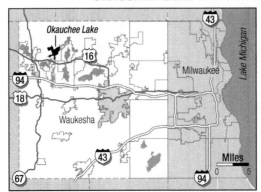

Okauchee Lake

43

16

Milwaukee

Lake Michigan

94

18

Waukesha

43

67

94

Miles
0   5

OKAUCHEE LAKE LORE:

"I've taken 6-pound bass out of Okauchee. It has trophy largemouth and smallmouth bass, walleyes, northerns and muskies. My personal view is that Okauchee Lake is going to become the best trophy musky lake in Wisconsin in the next 10 years."
— Don Streeter, guide

Acreage: **1,187**
Max. depth: **94** feet

FISH PRESENT

- ■ Walleyes
- ■ Northern pike
- ■ Muskies
- ■ Largemouth bass
- ■ Smallmouth bass
- ■ White bass
- ■ Rock bass
- ■ Perch
- ■ Bluegills
- ■ Crappies
- ■ Sunfish

◭ Private launch

◢ Public boat landing

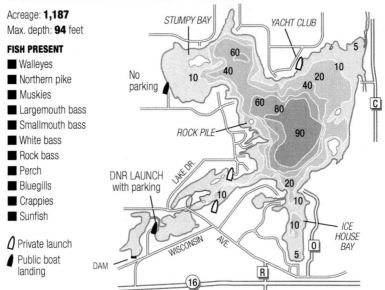

STUMPY BAY

YACHT CLUB

No parking

ROCK PILE

DNR LAUNCH with parking

LAKE DR.

WISCONSIN AVE.

DAM

ICE HOUSE BAY

16

C

R

0

Okauchee Lake

OKAUCHEE—That steady, gentle wobble you get when reeling in a deep-diving crank bait was interrupted by a sudden lightening-bolt tug that jolted up the line, through the rod and into my wrists.

I set the hook, then picked up the reeling pace because it felt like the fish was torpedoing toward the boat.

In the next instant, a musky materialized at boat-side, right there in front of me.

All I saw was a silver flash, a toothy grin and a quick tail-surge as the powerful fish spit the lure like a watermelon seed and vanished into the murky depths.

Don Streeter and I had been fishing the deep weed line for bass, but Okauchee Lake can be full of surprises.

Streeter is a guide and tournament angler. He is also past president and founding member of the Okauchee Fishing Club, which is named for the lake.

"We picked that name because Okauchee Lake offers every possible species and type of fishing," Streeter told me. "I mainly fish for bass and muskies, but the lake has all the game fish and panfish. It also has all types of structure—shallow bays with lily pads and surface weeds, deep weeds, rock bars, rocky points. It's a great lake to learn on because you can try so many different fishing techniques."

Okauchee, a 1,187-acre lake in northwestern Waukesha County with a maximum depth of 94 feet, is an all-species lake.

The DNR maintains a public boat launch on Highway T, off Wisconsin Avenue on the southwest side; and the Golden Mast restaurant, W349-N5253 Lacy's Lane, also has a private launch. There are no boat rentals.

"It's a hard lake to fish because the weed lines are so irregular," Streeter said. "You can't troll the weed edge effectively, and those weeds make lots of places for fish to hide."

As a result, the lake can produce some big fish.

"I've taken six-pound bass out of Okauchee," Streeter said. "It has trophy largemouth and smallmouth bass, walleyes, northerns and muskies. My

Don Streeter holds a largemouth bass caught in the weeds at Okauchee Lake.

personal view is that Okauchee Lake is going to become the best trophy musky lake in Wisconsin in the next ten years."

Sue Beyler of the DNR agreed that Okauchee has tremendous musky potential.

"Okauchee Lake has consistently produced some nice muskies," she said. "There's a good forage base and good habitat. There could be some real monsters out there."

The DNR has been stocking muskies since 1981. The annual quota is about 2,300 musky fingerlings. But Beyler said: "We've stocked as many as five thousand some years."

In the past, the DNR has also stocked walleyes.

"I think we need to do further study to see whether we should continue to stock walleyes," Beyler said. "There is a fishable population of walleyes and good gravel and cobble spawning habitat along the eastern shore. Sometimes stocking can hurt natural reproduction."

Beyond that, Beyler said, Okauchee has healthy, naturally reproducing populations of largemouth and smallmouth bass, northern pike, bluegills, perch, crappies, white bass, rock bass and sunfish.

The lake also has large populations of boaters and water skiers, so the best fishing time is probably on weekdays or evenings.

Streeter and I set out one humid, drizzly weekday evening in August when the lake was pretty quiet. We launched at the DNR ramp and motored over to Stumpy Bay on the lake's northwest side to work plastic lures in the shallows for bass.

We didn't find them there, so we switched to running spinners and crank baits in deeper water and started to catch a few fish.

"Because of the variety of structure on Okauchee Lake, at any given time, you can find fish in as little as a foot of water to as deep as 20 feet," Streeter said.

We found a mixed bag of fish at various structures and depths. We ended up catching and releasing a northern in shallow weeds, a few largemouth bass in the deep weeds, a bluegill next to a pier, plus a rock bass and one feisty smallmouth bass near a rock pile in fairly shallow water.

"Smallies will hang around rocks to feed on crayfish," Streeter explained.

Our best action—with that musky, plus some largemouth bass—came when the boat was over about 20 feet of water and we were casting deep-diving crank baits along the outside of the weeds at about 17 feet.

It wasn't easy because, with that jagged weed line, half the time you were hooking weeds. But, when your lure ran true, every now and then another fish might strike.

LAKE WINGRA/DANE COUNTY

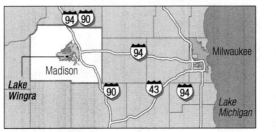

Acreage: 345
Max. depth: **21** feet

FISH PRESENT
- Muskies
- Largemouth bass
- Northern pike
- Black crappies
- Bluegills

LAKE WINGRA LORE:

"Without a doubt, it is one of the best musky action lakes in Wisconsin."
— Kurt Welke, DNR

Public boat launch
Carry-in boat launch

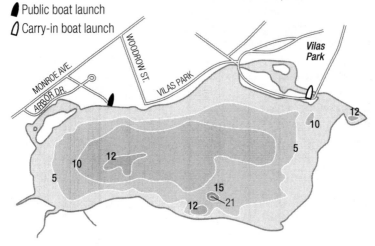

Lake Wingra

MADISON—We'd been on the water an hour or so, dragging a sucker beneath a bobber and working an assortment of musky baits along the outside weed line on Lake Wingra's north shore.

Charlie Grimm was throwing something that looked like a salamander made out of yellow plastic—he called it a "creature bait"—when a fish slammed it and he set the hook.

The pole bent in half as Grimm reeled and got the musky all the way up to the side of the boat.

We saw the quicksilver flash of a broad flank as the musky, with one powerful stroke of its long tail, somehow spit the hook and vanished in the general direction of the weeds.

"That one was probably in the mid-30s," said Grimm, staring at the place where the musky used to be.

According to Kurt Welke of the DNR, Lake Wingra is loaded with muskies that size, and up to about 39 inches long.

"Without a doubt, it is one of the best musky action lakes in Wisconsin," Welke said.

In fact, Lake Wingra has close to four muskies per acre.

"It has an adult musky density approaching four fish per acre," Welke he said. "That's four times what a good musky lake in Wisconsin would have."

The impressive musky numbers are the result of years of stocking and a special regulation that sets the daily bag limit for muskies at one fish, 40 inches or longer.

Although the number of anglers releasing legal-sized fish has increased in recent years, Welke said: "A lot of fish get removed when they reach 40 inches." As a result, DNR crews tend to see lots of muskies from 30 to 39 inches long and weighing 11 to 14 pounds when they do fish surveys, he said.

All of the muskies are stocked. Records show that musky stocking took place as long ago as 1979, Welke said. But, from about 1988 to 1996—sometimes with the help of local musky clubs—the lake received consistent stocking of as many as two muskies per acre per year.

That is what resulted in the current abundance, Welke said.

Charlie Grimm patiently waits for a musky to bite while trolling on Lake Wingra in Madison.

From an angler's perspective, there's probably no such thing as too many muskies. But, from a fish manager's point of view, Wingra has reached the point where enough is enough.

"Any angler would be happy to catch one of these muskies and have as much potential for action as you get on Wingra," Welke said.

But, he explained: "You've got a lot of muskies competing against their brothers and sisters for food resources. They're quality fish. But some anglers may want the opportunity to catch bigger, bulkier fish."

He characterized Wingra muskies "torpedoes, not tunas."

"What we'd like to see is some more fish a little bit heavier for their length," he said. "We need to bring that density down to one to two fish per acre."

To that end, beginning in 2002, the DNR has reduced the musky stocking quota for Wingra to one fish per acre every other year, and may consider further reductions, depending on the results of future fish surveys.

Wingra is a 345-acre lake with a maximum depth of 21 feet. The City of Madison operates a boat launch at Wingra Park on the north side of the lake. The daily launch cost will increase from $5 to $6 next spring.

The Wingra Canoe and Sailing Center, near the launch, rents canoes and rowboats from May through September. The cost is $10 for the first hour, $20 for a half-day, and $30 for a full day. There is also a carry-in launch, suitable for canoes and small boats, in Vilas Park on the northeast end of the lake.

A city ordinance requires slow, no wake boating on weekdays and no motors on weekends.

It addition to the muskies, Wingra has naturally reproducing populations of largemouth bass, bluegills, black crappies and sunfish, plus a few northern pike.

Welke, who grew up in Madison, remembers Wingra as a better bass lake a few years back. "We don't see the number of large bass that we'd see 15 years ago," he said.

Welke associates the decline of the bass with the rise of the musky population.

Despite its urban location, Wingra's shoreline includes the University of Wisconsin's arboretum, a zoo and parkland that afford both a natural setting and public access.

"There's lot of public access for shore fishing," Welke said. "Where else is Wisconsin can you walk down to a lake on a lunch break and catch three muskies?"

Because most of the lake is relatively shallow, the entire lake can hold muskies.

When my son, Rob, and I met up with Grimm one November afternoon, we concentrated our efforts on the outside of the weeds along the north and east shores. Later, we tried trolling crank baits out in the middle for a while. But, after that first musky, we weren't able to raise another one.

FOWLER LAKE/WAUKESHA COUNTY

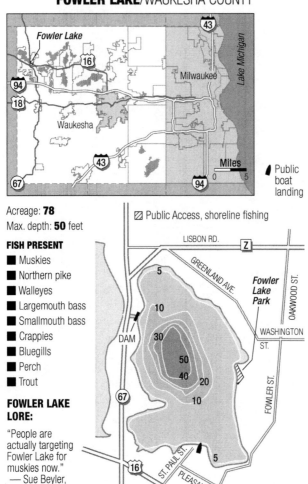

Public boat landing

Acreage: 78
Max. depth: 50 feet

FISH PRESENT

- Muskies
- Northern pike
- Walleyes
- Largemouth bass
- Smallmouth bass
- Crappies
- Bluegills
- Perch
- Trout

FOWLER LAKE LORE:

"People are actually targeting Fowler Lake for muskies now."
— Sue Beyler, DNR

Public Access, shoreline fishing

Fowler Lake

OCONOMOWOC—We were casting big musky baits along an outside weed line in the late afternoon sun, when I heard the unmistakable sound of musky induced excitement in Steve Miljat's voice.

"There's a follow," he yelled from his end of the boat.

I looked over and down just in time to catch a quick glimpse of a long, golden-bronze sub-surface form cruising silently up to the boat in hot pursuit of a crank bait. When Miljat worked the lure in a figure-8 pattern, the hefty fish turned, displaying a wide and powerful girth before giving up the chase and heading for the depths.

The scene took place—not on Pewaukee or Okauchee or some other longtime musky producing lake—but on little Fowler Lake in beautiful downtown Oconomowoc.

Until recently, Fowler Lake was known mainly for largemouth bass, walleyes and panfish. A copy of the DNR's book Wisconsin Lakes from 1991 doesn't even list muskies among the fish species found in Fowler Lake.

But things have changed.

"It has become a musky lake all on its own without any help from us," said Sue Beyler of the DNR.

Surprising Development

In about 1998, Beyler said, she started getting reports of anglers catching muskies on Fowler.

"I don't think people thought that little Fowler Lake would have muskies until they started to pick them up accidentally," she said. "But word has gotten around in the past few years. People are actually targeting Fowler Lake for muskies now."

The DNR doesn't stock muskies in Fowler Lake, Beyler explained. The muskies stock themselves.

Steve Miljat holds a small northern pike that hit a big musky lure on Fowler Lake, which is located in downtown Oconomowoc.

"They're coming down from Okauchee Lake and they're doing very well," Beyler said. "The muskies that I've seen (from Fowler Lake) have been nice healthy ones. You don't see any skinny ones. I've heard of muskies being caught in the upper 40s (inches)."

Fowler Lake is just 78 acres with a maximum depth of 50 feet. But it's part of the Oconomowoc River chain, which is made up of Pine, North, Okauchee, Oconomowoc, Fowler and La Belle lakes.

The DNR stocks 2,500 six- to eight-inch muskies in Okauchee Lake each year, and the Muskies Inc. club stocks another 300 12- to 14-inch muskies. The muskies migrate throughout the chain.

"It's pretty interesting that these fish want to travel like that," Beyler said. "They're really spreading out. I think it would be interesting to do a radio tagging to see where they're going."

The DNR also stocks 3,900 two-inch walleye fingerlings in Fowler Lake every other year. The lake also has naturally reproducing populations of largemouth and smallmouth bass, northern pike, bluegills, sunfish, perch, crappies and bullheads.

In addition, each spring the DNR stocks about six thousand "keeper" size trout—three thousand browns and three thousand rainbows—to provide some early season trout fishing, Beyler said.

The City of Oconomowoc operates a public boat landing with parking on the south end of the lake. The launch cost is $5. There are no boat rentals, but there is shore fishing access from a boardwalk near the launch and at Fowler Lake Park on the east shore.

Miljat and I fished Fowler Lake on a sunny June afternoon. It was the first trip to the lake for both of us.

Bass, Musky Caught

Because Fowler is a clear-water lake, Miljat said: "It's probably best to fish it during low light periods—dawn and dusk—or on cloudy days."

We concentrated our efforts on the outside weed line, working our way around the small lake twice, with musky baits and with bass baits.

"I'm impressed with the diversity of structure for such a small lake," said Miljat, a musky guide who spends most of his time on Pewaukee Lake. "It's not just a bowl. There's a steep drop off on the northwest end, some large weed flats and current from the Oconomowoc River."

For bass, we used medium spinning gear to throw plastic worms, tube jigs or small crank baits. Those methods produced one largemouth bass in the 13-inch range, plus a small northern pike, both of which we released.

When we switched to musky gear, throwing bucktails or big crank baits, things got more interesting. We caught and released two more small northerns, about 20 and 24 inches long. But what really got our attention was the sight of two different, good-sized muskies following our baits, about an hour apart.

"The first musky was 40 to 42 inches and the second one was in the mid-30s," Miljat estimated. "Those are two quality fish. I'll definitely be back."

That goes for me, too.

OCONOMOWOC LAKE/WAUKESHA COUNTY

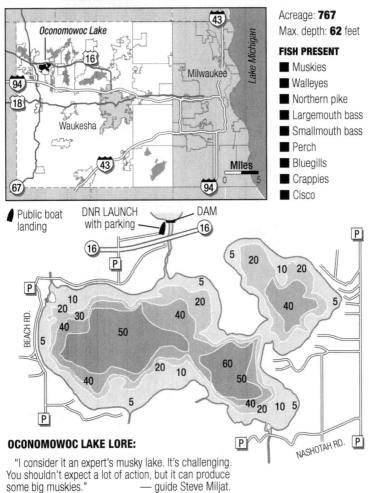

Acreage: **767**
Max. depth: **62** feet

FISH PRESENT

- Muskies
- Walleyes
- Northern pike
- Largemouth bass
- Smallmouth bass
- Perch
- Bluegills
- Crappies
- Cisco

Public boat landing

DNR LAUNCH with parking

DAM

Miles
0   5

OCONOMOWOC LAKE LORE:

"I consider it an expert's musky lake. It's challenging. You shouldn't expect a lot of action, but it can produce some big muskies." — guide Steve Miljat.

Oconomowoc Lake

OCONOMOWOC—For years, Oconomowoc Lake has been one of my favorite local lakes to fish for bass and walleyes.

Now I can recommend it for one more reason. It's the place where I caught the biggest musky of my life.

It happened on a cool, overcast June day that felt more like fall than spring.

Steve Miljat and I had been casting and reeling musky baits all morning long and were starting to think about giving up on the muskies and going after some smallmouth bass.

It's a good thing we didn't because, on the next cast I hooked into a monster musky and, after a hard-fought, twenty-minute battle, we got it into the net.

At four feet long and 28 pounds, this big fish was, for me, the culmination of a lifetime of musky fishing. I'd always hoped to catch one like it some day, but I really didn't think it would happen on Oconomowoc Lake.

"Oconomowoc has emerged as a musky lake since the mid-1990s," said Sue Beyler of the DNR.

Although muskies were never stocked in Oconomowoc, they get into the lake by "flopping over the dam from Okauchee Lake," Beyler said.

The DNR first learned that Oconomowoc Lake had a viable musky population during a survey in 1994. At that time, they estimated the musky population at 90 to 100 fish, but Beyler believes the number is increasing.

"In 1994, walleyes were the number one game fish sought after by Oconomowoc Lake anglers," she said. "Now it's probably switching toward muskies as people become more aware of them."

Even so, Oconomowoc may not be the best choice for a beginning musky angler.

"I consider it an expert's musky lake," said Miljat, a guide who has fished the lake for more than 20 years. "It's challenging. You shouldn't expect a lot of action, but it can produce some big muskies."

Part of the difficulty is the lake's extremely clear water.

"The old adage—'if you can see the fish, the fish can see you'—applies to Oconomowoc," Miljat said. "Because the water is so clear, it's best to fish at night or on rainy, overcast days."

Even then, a stealthy approach, long casts and light line (for species other than muskies) are all good ideas.

Oconomowoc is a 767-acre lake with a maximum depth of 62 feet. There are no boat rentals, but there is a public boat landing off the Highway 16 frontage road, east of Highway P.

You launch into the Oconomowoc River and head downstream for about three-quarters of a mile to the lake. It's a scenic ride, but the river twists and turns and has a few shallow spots that can cause problems, especially for big boats.

Unlike so many local lakes that are lined with a home or cottage every 50 feet, Oconomowoc has many large compounds and huge mansions.

The effect is a quiet lake with fewer piers, less shoreline development and less boat traffic.

In addition to the muskies, the lake has self-sustaining populations of smallmouth and largemouth bass, bluegills, crappies, rock bass and white bass.

Since 1995, the DNR has stocked about 2,300 northern pike fingerlings a year, plus 76,700 walleye fingerlings every other year. The lake also has cisco and white sucker populations that provide an excellent forage base for the muskies.

Another lake characteristic is limited weed growth.

"Weeds are at a premium," Miljat said. "Much of the lake bottom is sand and gravel. So, where you find weeds and rocks, chances are, you will find fish."

For smallmouth bass, Miljat recommends casting a spinner, small crank bait or tube jig into rocks and weeds in 8 to 9 feet of water.

The north shoreline is generally good for largemouth bass; some man-made fish cribs on the west end often hold largemouth and smallmouth bass; and a series of sunken islands in the east bay can hold all species.

The DNR survey, conducted in fall of 1994, found good concentrations of smallmouth bass at the fish cribs and walleyes in the narrows leading to the east bay.

For walleyes, there is a special 18-inch size limit with a daily bag limit of three.

Oconomowoc Lake

OCONOMOWOC—The Chippewa call it "ugly fish," but those of us afflicted with the fever see real beauty in even the most fleeting glimpse of the freshwater monarch known as the muskellunge.

How many times have we stood in taverns or sporting goods stores to stare at the sharp, white fangs and crimson gills of one of these mounted monsters and dared to dream?

There's a certain mystique, especially when this wily, serpentine predator attains massive, bulky flanks and a set of toothy, almost alligator-like jaws.

Look deep into its cold, carnivorous eyes and you might even find the stuff of which north woods legends, boyhood dreams and grown-up compulsions are made.

Some will never understand why anyone would be foolish enough to waste long, unproductive hours in pursuit of "the fish of ten thousand casts."

But hook into just one of these solitary mayhem machines, feel for an instant its awesome power, and you may begin to know why some develop an addiction to musky hunting.

It starts with a natural curiosity, fascination and maybe a little awe. Then, if you're not careful, it may soon accelerate into an irrational, irresistible impulse to pursue this king of freshwater fish.

The truth is, a musky addict makes playing the lottery look like an even bet. Without giving it a second thought, he is willing to gamble a season of frustration against the longshot chance of catching a big one.

Or The Big One.

What makes this business so tricky is the fact that a musky is a totally unpredictable fish.

One day, it may coil and, with a powerful stroke of its tail and a quick chop of its vice-grip jaws, strike suddenly at its prey, or a lure resembling it.

Or, after gorging, a musky may become inactive for days at a time, resting and digesting, virtually impervious to all temptation, even from a brand new $15 lure.

Bob Riepenhoff finally lived his musky dream, catching this 4-foot, 28-pounder in Oconomowoc Lake.

How can you tell when a musky will bite?

Volumes have been written speculating on the subject. But the way I see it, if you find the answer to that one, you will have solved one of the major riddles of the universe.

Maybe it has something to do with the weather or the moon phases. Maybe the planets have to come into alignment. Maybe fortune has to smile down on you.

I'm not really sure if there was a cause-and-effect relationship with any of those forces, but on a cool, cloudy spring morning, I caught the biggest musky of my life.

It happened on the choppy waters of Oconomowoc Lake, where I was fishing with my friend, musky guide Steve Miljat.

It was late morning when I made one more long cast, gave the jerk bait a tug, felt a hard slam and set the hook. There was brick-wall resistance, so I set the hook again.

This time, I felt a head-shake, a powerful surge and a long run. All I could do was hang on.

All of a sudden, the fish shifted gears and rushed the boat, so I had to reel as fast as I could.

The musky came up, affording my first glimpse of its massive head and long, bronze flank before vanishing with a quick stroke of its mighty tail.

That's when I felt the adrenaline start to pump through my veins.

For close to 20 minutes, the big fish put on an amazing display of strength and endurance with a series of jarring runs, hard dives, head-banging shakes and quick shifts in direction that left no doubt as to who was in control.

Thank God there were no jumps or rolls, or this story might have a different ending.

Four different times, I was able to gain enough line to work the big fish to the side of the boat and the fight seemed nearly won. But, each time, the musky erupted with yet another powerful surge and the battle continued.

The fifth time around, I lifted with all my might and was finally able to guide the musky into the net in Miljat's hands. It was four feet long and weighed 28 pounds.

And then it was over. I'm not just talking about that particular battle.

Sometimes we dare to dream big dreams. For years, I had one about catching a musky, 25 pounds or better, some day. The dream started a quest that lasted close to 30 years.

It ended that day on Oconomowoc Lake.